AMNESTY

AMNESTY

Saheera Thangal

Corporate Office:
EMPTY CANVAS PUBLISHERSTM
4435-36/7, 1st Floor
Ansari Road, Daryaganj
New Delhi-110002
Email: emptycanvaspublishers@gmail.com

Registered Office:
EMPTY CANVAS PUBLISHERSTM
AP-119C, Pitam Pura
New Delhi-110034 (India)
Email: emptycanvaspublishers@gmail.com
www.emptycanvaspublishers.com

Edition : 2023

ISBN: 978-93-90594-28-3

AMNESTY
Saheera Thangal

Published by:
EMPTY CANVAS PUBLISHERSTM
New Delhi-110034 (India)

Printed and Bound in india by Thomson Press India Ltd.

If you really exist, make me happy.
I don't believe the truth unless you make me happy.
I don't want to be dejected, humiliated and
abandoned anymore.
Prove me, you exist.

WITH GRATITUDE

For the strange relationships, even if they don't talk to you for years, you will be there for them forever. Ignatious Shaju Boustin, my best friend, thank you for filling the dots whenever I felt, "I don't know" at the beginning of AMNESTY.

Thank you to my little editor Ammu, my daughter who always gets cross with me when I call her by her real name 'Jalwa', for editing my novel beautifully with an artistic mind.

I am so happy and proud to call myself her 'mom'!

For the critics at home - younger daughter Kenza, and sister Sifa, who pinpointed even the smallest mistakes.

Thank you to my Publisher, Empty Canvas Delhi, who greatly supported me up to the last minute of editing, proof reading and publishing.

Mr Mansoor Cheruppa, working with leading publishing houses as a freelance designer for years, who has designed the book cover for Amnesty and made the readers fall in love with the first look itself!

A big thank you to my dear friend and well-known publisher in Delhi, MrJ.C Menon who encouraged me and extended his support with a loving heart.

I am grateful to JW Coetzee, Sudha Murthy, Marquez, Paulo Coehlo who taught me , language is the most magnificent companion to wander with your vagabond soul.

My family, friends in Middle east and India, readers and senior writers who have motivated and stood by me constantly.

And to Allah Almighty who gifted me a miracle and showed me how to detach from the darkness unknowingly!

To my Uppa, who made me understand how a Father should be and shouldn't be.

1

"I can't understand why you are still defending him?"

Bob was getting a little impatient when he asked this time. He already had asked the same thing at another occasion , but in a different aspect and tone.

"Bob, I know it's not that..."

"If it's not just skin deep, don't you think this is the right time to tie the knot?"

"Why does this 'proposal' thing always come in between?"

"You love him Alphy...But does he? He just needs you"

"Bob, have you ever seen your wife's eyes sparkle when you make love?"

"That's not the issue here..." Bob shook his head vigorously.

"It matters Bob, it definitely matters. A woman is always longing for that sparkle in her man's eyes. If it's only skin deep, you wouldn't find it..."

"So what are you trying to prove? After twelve years of happy marriage, Sheaba has mere bodily craving from me?"

"I won't say that" Alphy sighed.

I just wanted to talk about him; and his feelings for me. Ayaan is a mix of unconventional love"

A moment of silence creeped into their argument.

No one can answer why I have the burning desire towards him, even if it's the thousandth time! Why do I feel unsullied every time he kisses me on my bare neck?

Alphy's thoughts wandered carelessly.

Bob heaved his gaze towards the greedy horizon, through the French window of his office balcony.

It's amazing! I know the relationship between Alphy and Ayaan is just a typical one. Still my mind is blank. I know how a man's mind works in such situations. He won't let the girl go, he won't hold her either.

Bob was quiet when she left the cabin. He had work panned for the whole night.

He wanted Sheaba, Bob's wife and Alphy's preeminent friend , who would be happy pondering over her shadows and elusiveness."

Bob Justin. The man behind Bob Creations - the coveted creative firm for business tycoons!

The top creative head by bliss. They call him the 'Great Lord' of their products' subsistence.

2

Alphy is driving her car across Jumeirah Road from Media city , Dubai. This is one of the most charming moments in Alphy's life. She enjoys her solitude as she cruises through her positives and negatives.

Dubai - 'The City of happenings' always widen her roads for those who want to conquer the impossible.

She had lost her job in the past week. A reporter's job in the Face of Dubai newspaper is not child's play. Alphy, a thirty-two year old, is matured enough to understand that. She has been working in the same industry for five years. Her post graduation in Journalism and Mass communication from Bangalore journalist's college, and two years experience with a multinational magazine as a junior journalist at Bangalore gave her ample time to explore the media world and discover an identity of her own.

She didn't even think twice when her college friend Sheaba called her about the job opportunity at Face of Dubai . She laughs each time that scene comes into memory.

'Alph, catch a flight for coming Saturday. You are called for an interview by FOD. You will get the job, even Bob said so...'

"Bob said so..." is the exact phrase to define Sheaba.

That was it. Alphy, the enthusiastic, optimist who believed in her dreams, moved to Dubai from her home city Bangalore.

Her one and only Mom along with Aunt Reenu,

mama's sister, were at the airport to see her off. She couldn't see more than two drops of tears in mama's eyes. Period! Not one more drop than that.

She smiled.

Jumeirah beach!

Rearview mirror of her VW Polo is inquisitively peeping into her face.

Why all those arguments at Bob's place? I was defending a person who disappears at will and doesn't even bother about it.

Why my mind is reluctant to accept the reality or at least give a little space for Bob's ESP?

Alphy took a deep sigh and lowered the window to see the waves. It seemed like the thick, grey clouds are trying to obscure the colour from her. She stopped the car in the emergency lane of the busy road at Jumeirah 1.

People were jogging on the beautifully paved rubberised jogging tracks on the beach shore. Alphy got a little anxious when she saw kids roller skating, twisting and turning on their skates effortlessly. Even the smaller ones had good balance. Teenagers and adults were cycling towards the sea pier and returning to the point where they First started. A girl was arguing with her father or may be uncle, about the laps they had covered.

Alphy saw couples sitting on the beach bench. Some of them were laid back and leaned on their partners shoulders. Some were in their bikinis and trunks laying on the shore with their eyes closed.

A girl was sitting in the balcony of her glass villa which was on the opposite side of the road was looking at the palm trees in her villa compound. Occasionally she glanced at the waves.

Alphy closed her eyes and took a deep breath of fresh sea air.

Heart aches, it feels heavy too. But he doesn't understand.

She thought about the day when Ayaan told her about the colour less colour of the tides. It was just after the sunset. She was thrilled and uttered louder, 'It's true Ayaan, I can't make out the colours. There are millions!'

Ayaan kissed her lips and whispered, 'You got the same enchanting beauty all over your body ya habeebi; just after we invent each other in bed.'

Do you see the waves dancing and thrusting their folds to show love to the sun? Begging him not to set?

'Ayaan, why are you doing this to me? Leaving me for your own sake?

Can't you hear me?' Alphy's weep crashed inside.

Ayaan was right. She resembles the waves. Even when her deep insides roar, she pretends to keep her cool. The most priceless treasures are deep down, but the value depends on the diver who fetches the finest.

What if he was satisfied with the stones and pebbles? The huge difference between her and the waves; they are still able to cry for the setting sun.

Alphy, the accomplished journalist who lost her job last week for the most stupid reason in the world, couldn't even call her man's name louder.

Sheaba's most fascinating quality is that she never misses an opportunity to prepare a tasty cup of coffee. First cup; for Bob. Another two cups; one for her and one for Alphy.

Bob has an apartment near his office. It was in Jabel Ali, an oasis in the desert. When we enter the apartment compound; metamorphosis happens! The seven story apartment is surrounded by plush, green man-made hills. A lot of peacocks were wandering over the hills, calling out to their pair with a loud voice and dancing feathers.

Bob goes there whenever he needs to vent or meditate and be in solitude, away from the stressful advertising world. Make his headspace at peace before a long campaign.

Sheaba never complained.

Athul, their four year old son , irritates Bob for not coming home every evening. He complains that all the dads of his kindergarten friend's return home in the evening.

Anu's dad is a doctor. Kruthik's dad is an architect. Jyothi's dad owns a huge shopping centre. Minu's mom is head nurse at a hospital. Jyothi's dad brings an assortment of gifts for her every evening, Athul added.

One fine Friday morning, Bob was carrying Athul on their way back from church. Cool winter breeze patting over Athul's hair.

Bob asked him,

"Athul, why don't you pray to Jesus to make you born as Jyothi's dad's son in your next birth?"

After Bob heard Athul's answer; he always made sure to reach home in the evening, even if it's late; just to give Athul a goodnight kiss.

"No daddy... You are the best dad in this world for me. Don't get hurt! I was just kidding..."

Athul wept at the last word.

"Hey journalist... Don't forget about Connector. Day dreaming is not a valid excuse to skip an interview for Dubai's top most Magazine! "

Sheaba kept coffee for Alphy on the bed side table and smiled.

Alphy returned from the balcony of the thirteenth floor of Al Moosa tower, in Sheikh Zayed Road, one of the posh residential streets of Dubai. The skyscrapers in the street were lined with the tallest twin tower building. Holiday inn hotel, Al Attar tower, Dusit Dubai hotel, Al Rosthamani tower, the spherical Etisalat office, were a few among them.

Sheaba had left for the kitchen. It's amazing how she can appear and disappear in no time! When Bob is at home Sheaba transforms into different roles within seconds. She cooks well, it's another amazing part of Sheaba. Back home, she was a girl, leading a life like a deva under utmost care and security of her four elder brothers and rich father.

Sheaba's mother is a contrast in the family. As a reputed college professor; she believes in strictness and punctuality. Her brothers and father listen and agree with her all the time.

But Sheaba, a perfect rebel in the family always was an exception. And luckily; she was protected by others from her mother's rebukes.

Sheaba used to say; all teachers and nurses possess one common peculiar trait. They always hold a stick and look at the world through their own spectacles. And worse part is, they won't listen to what others have to say.

3

The Connector Magazine isolated at the 1st phase of Dubai Media City. It's a green glass building in rectangular shape. Most of the radio and TV channels in Dubai are re-located to Media City as its a free zone ; no need of sponsor to get visa.

Alphy, in dark blue trousers and an ocean blue top, Ayaan's favourite, was heading to the spacious, tastefully decorated ground floor.

She saw the bonsai plants with large and ocean pebbles at ground floor lobby.

Teenagers were talking pleasantly inside a cafe and sip a huge glass of hot chocolates. Their cute micro skirts and lazy jeenie pants were really cute.

A large Magrudy book store was there in the sixth floor ; alphy really missed her reading days. She loved books. She spent hours for reading in her college days. Even though she got a vast friend circle at times she loved being alone ; with her books.

She loved classics , poetries and books of historical paints and sculptures. She is so addicted to J W Coetze's disgrace. She had read the same hundred times or even more .

Lift open to the nineteenth floor. Alphy liked the Connector's reception back drop; CONNECTOR ; capital letters of the magazine name in grey colour back ground is the logo, simple but attractive in an artistic way.

Receptionist asked Alphy to wait at the reception foyer , for sometime. Alphy looked outside through the huge glass wall. The vision was spectacular!

Cluster of huge buildings surrounded by artificially extended Jumeirah beach back waters. Cars moving like toys on the sheikh zayed road; over the flyovers.

Alphy entered the vast lobby of Connector and was guided to the Editor in Chief, Amit Gautham's cabin.

"So Alphy Ron, nothing more we need to know! We are looking forward to having you in our Connector family!"

"Thank you Mr. Gautham, the pleasure is mine."

"And a very confidential and challenging task I am assigning you for. That's the only screening process at Connector!"

Alphy smiled and listened. In fact, she was well aware of the procedure and was curious about the assignment she is going to take up. All credit goes to my best buddy Bob, who was well versed with the pulse of media world.

"Dubai , the City of Gold , has another life behind the veil. I have been investigating about this for a long period. The truth is the Dubai authority still does not know about those lives, the people residing in the country illegally for years." Alphy in fact, became disheartened when Bob revealed about Connector's mystery mission and onus they entrusted to a new employee to evaluate their efficiency. She had hoped for a lot more.

What's so exciting about this? The whole world has illegal immigrants. Ultimately who gets to decide some humans can stay and some can't ?

Who created these maps to find routes and who asked to keep borders and territories? People born in this world without their knowledge need an identity card to prove their existence? Absurd!

Alphy thought about Garry Davis and his concept of world passport and one government.

Amit gautham smiled, then got up from his chair and asked her to follow him.

There is a revolving shelf, full of different coloured files and some of them are protruding from it.

The one which Amit opened and closed in front of her eyes excited her right away and she shook hands with him.

She agreed and signed a contract of Dhs.20,000 per month to investigate an extraordinary story of a family who is residing somewhere in the UAE for years, illegally.

Alphy either has to fulfil her agreement, or quit.

4

Rain!

It is the most beautiful art in the desert. Alphy couldn't resist herself to open her senses the fullest, just to savour the smell of the virgin rain!

She was about to get into her car at the parking lot when another car speeded across, splashed the water, almost hit her and stopped right next to her.

She was pulled into the car by a masculine hand. Alphy's scream dissolved into the thunder. He hugged her drenched body tightly before she could make out his face.

'Why did you wear this blue? You ignite me '

Alphy gasped for a brief moment. Ayaan passionately spread her over and kissed her wet body's peaks and valleys. She was gushing like a river, and he drained every bit.

'Ayaan's coupe'

That is the name of his villa at Palm Island - a man made island. From the sky, the archipelago resembles a stylised palm tree encompassed within a circle...

A beautiful two-storey villa perched on a private beach with a tall palm tree at the main entrance.

Each villa in Palm Island has its own compound, a corridor opening to the sea, and a yacht tied up right in front of their private sea entrance. It is the island for the world's elite.

It resembles the backwaters of Kerala, where small houses with private canoes adorn the banks. God's own country. Alphy recalled those Malayalam movies she watched at film festivals in Bangalore.

Alphy loves to swim in his private swimming pool. Ayaan always tempted her to explore the private beach. But she preferred the pool in the moon light and those deep, intense hugs while they swim.

"It's not as easy as you think habeebi..."

Alphy couldn't figure out exactly what Ayaan meant by that. And it came as a slight shock as well.

Everything under the sky is possible!

That's Ayaan. You can say that his positive charm makes him magnetic. Whoever drew close to him got stuck in that web.

But a fondly stuck butterfly I am.

Am I really stuck in it or am I staying ?

Alphy hugged Ayaan passionately. Ayaan's villa in the Palm Island became the perfect setting for their jam and butter bond.

Ayaan got up from the bed and walked to the balcony and lit his favourite cigar.

Alphy covered herself in Ayaan's comfy feather quilt and followed. He made her sit on his lap.

"Illegal immigrants are common in the Middle Eastern countries, but to find a family residing illegally for years in UAE..."

He shook his head skeptically...

Alphy asked him curiously, "Would it be that difficult?"

When Mr. Amit Gautham explained about the screening assignment Alphy was not even considering it as a challenge. A spirited journalist like her would dare to venture into uncharted territory. That's what excites her!

Why is it suddenly vexing her? Why am I nervous when this man says it's difficult ?

Ayaan hugged and kissed her bare shoulder passionately and whispered, «Sweet heart, I will definitely die for your shoulder." And he broadened her with his passion.

Ayaan fondly scratched her ears.

Alphy cherished this moment. Looking into his eyes. They became a world of oceans and mountains when he wanted to give her warmth. And Alphy unleashed the invisible chain that restrained her body and let go whenever she got hooked by those eyes.

Ayaan carried her to the bedroom in his arms, "Don't worry, those illegal immigrants you are looking for will be in front of my habeebi. Give me a week's time."

He teased her dainty, second ear piercing with his nose. Alphy's heart blushed with coyness. She spread around him and returned the heat and fire!

5

“A Road to Mecca.

Have you read that book?” Alphy asked.

Ayaan reduced the volume of his car’s stereo and looked at her.

“Come again?”

“Autobiography of Mohammed Asad; an Islamic scholar. A celebrated classic from the day it was born”

“I am Ayaan; not Asad my dear” he laughs ...

She looks at Ayaan with exasperation. Ayaan softly pokes her cheek and says,

“Ya Allah, I can’t still figure out which face of yours turns me wild.”

“That’s what you are. Don’t blame my face.” Alphy replies with an unabashed smile.

“Alph... Why don’t you write a book called Road to Fujjairah. In fact, this journey embeds a mystery. You felt that. Right?”

Alphy was amazed when she heard Ayaan. He was acting like he never knew Mohammed Asad, the classic author. A voracious reader like Ayaan would definitely know about him.

Ayaan started talking about the book.

The beginning of the road was extremely beautiful. Asad wanted to reveal not only his life, he moreover wanted to separate it from belief and convey to the world why there is religion.

What do you think Alph?’

“I don’t agree” argued Alphy. “Mohammed Asad beautifully harmonised the real world mannerisms to faith and religion. Men are indeed invaluable when they abandon themselves to surrender to the universe”

“You mean universal power? So what are you trying to say? If you don’t see or feel the presence of Allah, you are simply agreeing with Rhonda Byrne or Deepak Chopra? Aren’t you Alph?”

Alphy smiles at Ayaan.

“No, I didn’t mean that. In my view, universal power is God or we can call that as Allah, the omnipresent or Jesus, who surrendered himself to be crucified for the sin of mankind including you and me”

“Alph, let’s not talk about this topic”

He is a natural when it comes to switch subjects of conversation.

“What shall we talk about then? Desert and camels?” Alphy laughs.

Two people; from different religions and faith are madly in love with each other. A beautiful castle! Sometimes she fantasised about the light and swing in that castle. A beautifully adorned wooden bench in a garden of freshly scented flowers.

Alphy is certain about a day when Ayaan will join her, or she will follow his footsteps to that serenity.

6

Alphy gazed at the road curving and stretching like a snake towards Fujairah.

The road to Fujairah is an experience. Alphy longed for the journey to never end. Mountains adorned with boulders showcased their architectural marvel proudly. There is nothing other than endless mountains on either sides of the road. Sometimes the roads leap only to a fall, like a winding roller coaster.

Alphy is really stunned and held his shoulder tightly when she couldn't see the road while turning a sharp bend.

Seems like diving into the sea.

Ayaan touched Alphy's chin and whistled.

"This is the beach Alph. The most beautiful beach in UAE. Korfaqaan!"

Ayaan had kept his promise. He had a vague idea about the location of the family residing in Fujairah; one of the beautiful coastal areas of United Arab Emirates.

Bob was planning to accompany her on this trip. Everything went as planned till yesterday. Then came Ayaan!

He was totally out of the picture for the past three weeks or so.

Ayaan's mobile ringer will be on only if he needs the call. And he will answer only if he wants to.

Sometimes she doesn't even know why he is doing this. She tried day and night. Alphy couldn't even concentrate on anything including her job, which demands focus to capture imagination.

She heard her palpitation first time in her life.

Life is a horrible hill station. Even if we wait the whole day, a single train may not come.

Ayaan dug a hole in Alphy's heart. She felt the suffocation at times, as if there was no oxygen at all.

Greenery vanished. Colour, smell, taste. She felt like nothing existed.

A vacuum!

She cannot pedal her boat. It was shaking, twisting, in the middle of the sea, hardly moving along with the wind.

Then he appears another dark night. Her apartment's bell rings in the middle of the night and immerse her from the emptiness. Or a sudden call to her mobile after weeks or months, at times even more than that.

Alphy cried and yelled at him. She just needs a reason to make convince herself.

He keeps silent. No matter how hard she tries. Sometimes he gives her very silly reasons. Held up with an unexpected major project or forced to go for an emergency family meet back in Lebanon; or complicated legal matters in the company and so forth.

She doesn't understand the logic and emotion behind it. And how these matters really matter enough to not make a phone call or even a message. Even a default return message 'I m in a meeting', is enough for her to console herself.

Later, he promises her it will not happen again. And she forgets everything.

But the same loop will happen over and over again.

The same unanswered calls. Whenever she picks up her phone to make a call, she feels the heaviness in her heart. What would she do if he doesn't pick up? She feels helpless and tries to make sense of his logic.

He says that he enjoys it occasionally.

Really!! How can a person relish the pain of the another human? The one who thinks of him as her universe.

She tried to do the same in return, to keep a distance at least for a while. Avoiding his calls, messages and to not meet .

But it was just not practical with him. He was such a bloody heart who knew workings of Alphy's mind. He knows how to break her silence and how to re-connect with her.

Forgiving once misstep is the higher grade of humanity, especially when its come to love. Ayaan always took it for granted.

In that moment , Alphy recalls her argument with Bob. She still holds onto her faith.

She can't figure out who is the real victim here. Alphy with her contented love or Ayaan with his romantic ignorance.

Alphy realises that this love is not disruptive for her. It's going to be him who is unable to breathe if she stops loving him. And the amusing part is, he still doesn't know that.

Alphy finally gives in to the uncertainty and burning love of her soul.

And when they meet after the void, he whispers passionately and begs like a naughty child, 'I need you Alph. How can I be with you forever? What shall I do for that?'

Ayaan is a pearl-blue bounded book having infinite chapters. Alphy etched on every page with her eyes a thousand times. Even so, some pages are illegible. Some lines are chanting their distinct language. They are like an unpredictable chameleon.

Pain makes one a warrior in life! Pain which is unbearable out of love, makes one, mesmerisingly powerful.

7

The day following our night, Ayaan, as he had promised collected some valuable information about the illegal expatriates residing in Fujairah for over twelve years.

After which he vanished for his Austrian venture of a hotel designed like a ship; a one billion dollar project of his architectural firm, FORTELLO.

Poor Bob, who had postponed his urgent conference to join with Alphy, was ditched.

It is no surprise for Bob when Ayaan comes into the picture. He knows Alphy.

Alphy wonders how Bob gets into the psyche of people even if he doesn't have a personal relationship with them.

After a long three-hour journey from Dubai, they reached Korfaqaan in Fujairah. Alphy wondered how people would have travelled through the rough and roaring sea during the fifties, to reach the Gulf, that too without proper documents. They must have pleaded with death to spare them through the journey before reaching Korfaqan shore.

A man in long kandhura and taqiyah (cap) received them with a charismatic smile.

"Assalaamu alaikum yaa rafeeq. Ana Abdulla bin Abdul Kalaam"

Ayaan shook hands cheerfully and greeted back. "Va Alaikumussalamva rahmathullaahi vabarakaathu. I am Ayaan Muhammed Ali"

Alphy smiled at Abdulla and he welcomed her,

"Ahlan..ahlan"

Ayaan's boss owned a luxury beach apartment in Fujairah, which served as a holiday home. He visits whenever he feels like diving for new pearls to adorn, host weekend parties and then he retreats back to his busy routine.

FORTELLO is a multinational architecture and interior design company with branches across the world.

Ayaan's boss Mukthar Ahammed, is a fifty-five year old 'playboy' business tycoon from Lebanon. He has three wives and still dives for fresh pearls wherever he halts his private jet.

Mukthar has a little bit of patriotic spirit, hence most of his staff are from Lebanon, including Ayaan. Ayaan is the chief architect and his best buddy. Their intimacy sparked jealousy in the workplace towards Ayaan. But no one dared to express it directly.

8

They were following Abdulla through a narrow alley. Ayaan was walking with Abdulla. Alphy was following behind.

It seems like Abdulla knows the purpose behind their visit. The alley grew narrower and various residents were passing by. A group of teenagers in their long kurthas were sitting in an open air cafeteria and having Shawarma. Some of them were smoking hukkas and sharing the pipe with one another.

Alphy was noticing their khurtha colors. All were light, pastel colours. Pink, blue, ivory, white and grey, but looked like they were not washed for weeks!

They were noticing the strangers with Abdulla. Some of the middle aged men greeted Abdulla 'Khaifal aal..'

Ayaan, was walking with Abdulla and talking continuously about different matters including the latest change of rules in United Arab Emirates. They are making the labor laws stringent. The employee can now work only under their respective sponsor or will have to pay hefty fines. Thousands of labours are working in gulf countries, but not under their respective sponsors. They are recruited by agents who collect huge amounts of money for visas from them. Most of the employees don't even know their sponsors and in which emirate they belong to.

Visa rackets were responsible for the increasing number of illegal emigrants.

Alphy was watching Ayaan. She liked to observe

him all the time. The way he carries himself. Ayaan is tall and masculine. He doesn't like to work out for six packs, but opts for toned physique and fitness. He swims every day. He was a champion in swimming during his college days.

They walked almost one kilo meter through the interior road. Alphy was intrigued and surprised to see the interior alley roads and dusty, narrow footpaths. It reminded her of the alleys back in Bangalore.

She covered her hair, mouth and nose with her stole. When Ayaan looked back while talking with Abdulla, he saw Alphy in veil and that made him smile. He paused and slowed down his strides to reach Alphy.

"Sweet heart; you look really hot in veil."

Ayaan whispered to Alphy. Abdulla who was walking in front of them turned and looked back. Ayaan was pointing his fingers to the nearest grocery and pretended that he is asking her if she needs something from there.

She was thirsty actually. Ayaan asked Abdulla to wait for a while and went to the off-white, single shutter grocery. Alphy was standing in front of the grocery and closely observed the surroundings.

Kids were playing football near a huge waste bin; some of them were wearing kandhuras and the others in their unbuttoned shirts. Alphy tried to make out their language from their lip movements and gestures. She felt uncomfortable and confused about the thought she came across. Children are fundamentally innocent. No matter from where their ancestors are and which language they spoke. This place seemed like an ancient cave with lots of archeological foot prints. She could never imagine a place like this in United Arab Emirates.

Being a journalist, she always longed for utmost

freedom. Freedom to smile, cry, talk, express and dance in the rain! Freedom to eat what she likes and to dress elegantly occasionally. There are moments when she doesn't bother about food or her appearance.

She is a couch-potato in her room with careless shorts and t-shirts. But The City of happenings - Dubai, influenced her thought process these days. Being a prominent, fire-brand journalist, she cannot cling onto a narrow ideology of detesting democracy.

Dubai rulers and their kingdom coerced her to change her vision in darkened areas of life. People feel safe here. They don't kill other human beings in the name of food or religion. They don't keep women as slaves and don't limit their education. They don't force them to get married as soon as they reach puberty. Wives call their husbands by their names and the latter does not feel inferior about it.

9

Finally, they reached the villa of Raheem and Nabeesa; the illegal residents.

Raheem was not at home. Nabeesa didn't come out from the house for a long time. Abdulla rang the bell from the gate and waited.

In the outskirts of the city, villas are surrounded by a huge compound wall and gate, with a calling bell on the gate itself. Strangers are not allowed even in the compound wall without permission. That is the Arabic custom. They have peep holes on the gate. Alphy was thinking about back home in India, everyone can enter the house compound and ring the bell placed at the front door. Some houses keep dogs and others keep security guards at the gate.

Finally Abdulla knocked on the gate three times. He told Ayaan about the pass code. Nabeesa would not open the gate unless she hears the pass code. Raheem revealed this code to his very close friends. Abdulla is one of them.

Nabeesa was in panic. She opened the gate just enough to peek outside. She saw us with Abdulla and her face went paler. She asked Abdulla to leave. Abdulla informed Nabeesa that he had a chat with Raheem about the matter and that he had permitted to bring them.

Raheem got a stall at the fish market. It is his friend Junaid's business, and he helped the family to survive. Abdulla paged him, but Raheem didn't call back. They waited for little longer, and returned dejectedly.

Abdulla asked Ayaan and Alphy to stay in Fujairah for one or two days patiently, and he promised that he will talk to Raheem again.

They returned to Khorfaqan and stayed at Mukhthar's beach villa.

A Nigerian cook and Philippino house keeper were waiting for their arrival. Mukthar informed them to treat their guests cordially.

It was a plush villa. Elegant interiors made it more royal!

Alphy was exhausted. Ayaan took a bath and performed Namas. Dinner was ready by this time. Grilled chicken, mutton kabaab with soft, Arabic kubhoos, hummus and garlic paste along with clear soup and a fresh, Arabic vegetable salad were waiting for them on the dining table which looked over the terrace into the open sea. Ayaan went straight to bed after dinner.

10

Alphy sat on the couch near the window and watched the water reflect after the pink sunset. She could see the deep blue water through the French windows. It is low tide. Waves were hitting on the sea pier with gentle caresses. Alphy shifted her gaze to the black and white painted orderly cabin near the gate. It must be the security cabin. Alphy shifted her view further. A long road along the beach which suddenly steered into a U-turn, exclusively for the villa entrance.

Alphy felt the urge to talk to someone at that moment. Ayaan was fast asleep. She went downstairs. The staircase resembles the Mughal's grandeur. Long, curvilinear, and spacious. The Ground floor lobby of the villa looks sophisticated. Alphy never liked the bulky, wooden furniture. But traditional furniture of Arabs were heavy and mostly in dark woods. Darker toned wood is expensive and traps heat. Elaborate Islamic ornamentation and respect for aesthetics is another character. In order to achieve this, they used colossal arches, sweeping courtyards, and lavish lawns with numerous arcades and porticos.

They tailored the portico as a majlis with extravagant golden and cherry coloured fabric, floor cushions were spread around the perimeter to act as low seating. They maintained high quality in every nook and corner.

Alphy entered to an inner courtyard that served as centre of the house. As she walked through the long hallway, the Persian candle lit lamps lighted up the arches and columns which boasted of roman influence.

This could be seen in majority of the Arab villas. It must have originated during the 18th or 19th century. The hallway separates the front door from the courtyard, might be to discourage visitors from peeking into the private areas of the villa.

Alphy liked the long, soft, and lush rugs inside, covering the floor wherever she moves.

She reached the guard's quarters through the front door. She wondered where the cook and house keeper sleeps. She didn't want to disturb them, hence she opened and closed the front door softly.

The guard was sitting in his chair. He was wearing a balaclava, commonly called a monkey cap in India, and a dark green blazer. He saw Alphy approaching , and he came out from his cabin with a curious face and widened eyes as if he was expecting an emergency!

'Good evening ma'am, assalaamu alaikum. May I help you?' He asked.

Alphy smiled at him and said 'nothing to worry' in a hushed voice. 'Just thought to come and talk to you when I saw you from the balcony.'

'Oh...ok. No problem. Is everything fine here ma'am? Aap hamaara mehmaan hey. Mukthar Saab is very particular about his guests.' he paused and looked at her.

'Aap India se hey?'

'Yes.Where are you from?' She asked

'Kerala' , he replied.

'Oh...that's cool. I have been to Kerala several times. My friends are there in Cochin.'

His eyes sparkled for a moment!

'Thoppumpadi, my house is in Fort Cochin'.

And the next glance was in despair. Alphy noticed the change. She recognised that emotion. There was nostalgia or missing his dear ones.

'Aap ka naam kya hey? You speak English and

Hindi very well... '

'My name is Yousuf . I didn't go to school ma'am , I think any language can be easily learned if we are hungry. Life always wanted me to look after others, take over responsibilities, to feed my whole family was one among them. When I was at the age of fourteen, our baapa left my umma and eight children in a single-room thatch house; we call it a *koora* in Malayalam - small mud houses, the roof covered with large, dried coconut leaves , pleated like a girl's hair. Water leaked into the room whenever it rained.'

Yousuf smiled. Alphy was silent for a moment. Sometimes life plays games with us. Even if you have the finest vocabulary, you won't be able to utter one word.

11

'My dad was a sraank, the man who is controlling the Uru, or fat boat. The type of boat has been used by the Arabs since ancient times as trading vessels, and even now urus are being manufactured and exported to Arab nations from Beypore, the sea gate in Kozhikkode, ? '

Yousuf went to the Uru to feed nine bellies after his father left them. He explained they keep the newcomers as cooks initially. The cooking space in the Uru was hell on earth. A small, crammed space underneath the spiral staircase. There was no ventilation. You will feel like you are inside an oven when you light the furnace.

The other senior workers in the uru will find reasons to beat us. Sometimes it is about over-cooked meat, or uncooked meat. Even if the dish is absolutely fine they will find other reasons to ridicule and humiliate.

'Days are still better. I had prayed to Allah for the sun to not set. Darkness was the worst in that hell. They made us sexual slaves. Not one person, two or three will come and go. They abused us brutally. After a long ten years I became the sraank. But I never abused a single child. Rather, I saved them from others.

One day I heard news, from one of my teenage boy that recently joined, that the others are not comfortable with me and they are planning to get rid of me during my return journey from Korfaqaan.

I ended up here and said goodbye to my sea life

forever.

Mukthar sahib's father, Muhammed Salah gave me this job. Mukthar Sahib was ten years when I first met him. It has been long thirty-five years since I have been with them. After sahib's Abu passed away five years back, it has been just a holiday home for Mukthar sahib"

She felt sorry for him. She could not even imagine the brutality he had faced. She apologised for ruining his sleep. He smiled and replied that he wouldn't have slept even if she did not visit.

"I am the guard here. My job is to stay awake the entire night." He smiled.

Alphy bid good night to 'Yousuf' and returned to her room.

Getting rich is an unexplainable science!

People in the old days entered into gulf countries through *Uru* illegally. They later became multi-millionaire businessmen. And may be a few some that had travelled through the same *Uru*, are still guarding bungalows of Arabs, staying awake throughout the night.

12

The sense of disappointment faded away. Alphy went to take a bath taking her towel and night wear. She felt calm and more relaxed with a confidence to meet the family the next day.

After her bath, Alphy crawled inside Ayaan's comfy white quilt. Ayaan was sleeping, but subconsciously allowed her to cuddle closer, and his hands wrapped her tight. He started to snore. She smiled and kissed his arms.

She couldn't sleep.

Her thoughts were filled with the stream she saw in the middle of the desert. She knew about the oasis. The closer you get to it, the further it moves away.

Alphy was trying to recall the exterior of Raheem and Nabeesa's villa. It was absolutely deserted in the desert, surrounded by a few similar villas and an old, single shutter grocery shop with a faded yellow and green paint. It is run by a Pakistani. He was wearing a long kandhura and white embroidered cap and held a chant shackle. He was consumed in *thasbeeh and takes a break whenever a customer enters to purchase groceries. (**thasbeeh - praise the Almighty Allah)*

The villa's windows were almost broken. The steel frame of the window was lined with dust. There was a window AC on one side of the wall. The other AC hole is boarded with a thick, hardboard.

She was wondering how this stream appears in the desert. Abdulla says it's the peculiarity of the desert. You don't know when and where the camels or streams will materialise. It is like the scenery changes with a wave of a magician's wand. They have mystifying powers!

Alphy sensed that Abdulla would not be too keen on the geographical potential of the phenomenon.

She can feel the cold and warmth of the water against her feet. The water was crystal clear. When she walked forward , Ayaan accompanied her, along with his handy cam. He is such a nature lover. He describes everything like an artist. About the tree bark, smooth and sharp edges of leaves, softness of petals, scents of wild abode of flowers. He knew the speed of diverse birds and the sounds of the jungle! He elucidates the minuscule details of nature and people experience along with his voice.

Abdulla was warning them to be cautious. He said there might be sharp plants under water that can tear the skin.

Ayaan was clicking pictures of her movements. She came across a huge tortoise skeleton on the shore and called out to Ayaan. He came enthusiastically and took pictures. Alphy could see the precision of each rib of the skeleton. It was milky white and just perfect. How come the bones remain so unpolluted?

She wondered about the human skeleton. Would it be similar to this?

He laughed. Typical Ayaan.

"Alph, I can only see your milky white body and mesmeric skin. Each time I touch you, I feel attracted like a magnet.Trust me..."

"Am I a mere body to you?" she questioned relentlessly.

She was rather influenced with 'Bob vibes' in her mind.

Ayaan looked for Abdulla and noticed he was quite far away from them and was talking loudly on the phone. Ayaan took advantage of the moment. He hugged Alphy tightly and kissed her neck.

Alphy couldn't resist. For a moment she was frozen, but then pushed him away.

He was smiling again.

"Alph, you have told me numerous times that my body scent drives you wild, right?"

Alphy was quiet.

"You told me that you wanted to swallow me and keep me inside you forever"

Ayaan came closer,

"Then why are you differentiating body and soul? Suppose my soul abandoned my body, will you hug and keep me in your bed forever?"

Alphy looked at him with annoyance,

"That's not the question here."

" What else then? What exactly is your question ya habeebi?Why are you detaching your body from your soul? Body will turn frozen without a passionate soul. Think about it darling..."

Alphy was contemplating the contradictions between the perspectives of Bob and Ayaan.

She opened her eyes the following morning, when Ayaan woke her with a hot cup of coffee in his hands.

13

Alphy saw that Ayaan was sitting in the balcony which opened out to the sea. She freshened up and joined him on another sofa. His empty coffee cup was perched on the coffee table. He was going through the news paper 'Face of Gulf'.

"You would still be working there if you had accepted your MD's proposal, Isn't it darling? My silly foolish girl!" Ayaan laughed at her.

Alphy wasn't humoured.

Ayaan was in the mood of teasing her.

'Arman is handsome, powerful and wealthy. Why did you reject him Alph?'

"I didn't, I told him I don't want to marry a married man."

He laughed.

" Alph, you are in love with a Muslim. You should have modest awareness about the religion. Don't you know we can marry upto four?

'What do you mean by that? It's nothing to do with your religion and permission to have four wives. It's about self respect and dignity. Women would rather die than share her man.

Will you be okay if I keep multiple partners?'

Ayaan said YES immediately. Alphy stared in disbelief.

"You can, but I won't be there one of them" he added.

Alphy laughed. 'Oh, so that's your perspective. you handsome selfish...'

She teased him back. His eyes filled with tears.

Alphy sat on his lap and gently held his face to her chest. He was silent for a long time. She could feel his breathe - long, deep, intermittent. A woman goes soppy if she see a man's eyes filled. Are those tears of love or weakness?

'I was just kidding sweet heart...' She kissed his eyes.

'Well, don't. I don't like it...'

He whispered and squeezed her even more tightly. He was probing like an infant, who had awoken abruptly from a deep sleep.

14

The following day, the situation had drastically changed. Raheem was waiting for them in front of the compound wall, slightly far away from his villa's gate. That must be a precautionary action, due to his fear about his illegal identity. He greeted Alphy and Ayaan with a pleasant face. He apologised to them for the previous day.

Alphy replied that it was absolutely fine and they can completely understand their situation.

Raheem said, 'This is the last chance for me and my family to return to our home place. '

Alphy looked at Ayaan that instant, and he winked. She realised the whole situation. Ayaan must have told Abdulla we would help them to escape from this desert where they were enslaved for a decade.

Raheem asked Nabeesa to bring tea for the guests. Nabeesa's face turned paler. It seems like she was not very happy to narrate their story to strangers.

After tea, Abdulla left them with Raheem. He said he will return by evening.

Ayaan initiated the conversation;

"Abdulla said you are working in a fish market?

Raheem answered yes by nodding.

'I am a science graduate!' Raheem added with a peculiar smile. Alphy tried to figure out that odd smile. It may be a paradigm, stating that a science graduate never works in a fish market, or deserves something better in life. Look at me, where have I reached now?

"Life was perfect you know. Everything was moving smoothly.

Me, my wife and our first baby...

I was running a grocery in Umm Al Quwain situated in a wealthy Arab neighbourhood. Business were going very well with Allah's grace. I had been thinking to expand the business like every other entrepreneur.

As part of the expansion plan, I had leased an additional shutter and applied for visa to employ two more staffs from Kannur."

Raheem stopped mid-sentence and looked at Alphy and Ayaan.

'Hope you have heard about Kannur? Its in Kerala. It's our home place.'

Being a journalist Alphy definitely knew about Kannur, and their unstable political scenario. Ayaan smiled at Raheem and asked him to continue.

" My Arbaab was a good man. He had supported me whenever I requested. He agreed at first instance when I asked his permission for the expansion. But I don't know what changed when I approached him to sign my new employees' visa.

He demanded for an increase in his sponsor fee. I was totally zero by that time. Expansion plans had started and I invested every single Dirham into it. Luckily or unluckily the two men who were planning to come to work in my grocery agreed to pay five thousand dirhams each towards the visa expenses.

I wouldn't have taken that money if I could have managed the extra financial burden. Expansion was at the final stage, and I had to complete it and reopen my grocery within no time to recover my business.

I agreed with the sponsor to increase his sponsor fee. But I asked him to give me at least six months to nourish my expanded business and draw some income."

Ayaan and Alphy were looking at Raheem eagerly. In between the conversation, Nabeesa brought and served sulaimani in a tray. Alphy looked at her full stomach. It was almost touching on the coffee table when she laid down the tray. Her face was overly pale.

But she had very beautiful eyes with long eyelashes. Her hands were very thin and she was wearing a few glass bangles.

Nabeesa smiled at Alphy. Alphy smiled back.

'What then? Did he agree?' Ayaan was curious.

'No. he didn't. '

Raheem patted his half bald head in remorse. Alphy noticed the pain reflected in Nabeesa's eyes.

"He didn't agree and neither did he apply for the new employees' visa. I was shattered! I didn't have a single penny for my house expenses. My elder daughter was just 2 years old, We couldn't even buy her baby food...I didn't know a good man can switch to evil in a split second.

I asked for help from my friends and near ones. But everything had a limit. All of them were here to make some money for their beloved's living. Isn't it?

I tried to convince my sponsor in so many ways. He was not at all willing. He gave me two months time to pay his sponsor fee or he would take over the grocery from me!

15

Raheem needed to go to the fish market in between, as he got a pager to reach back urgently. He asked Alphy and Ayaan to sit and finish their sulaimani. Raheem asked Nabeesa to give them company.

Ayaan accompanied Rahcem. He wanted to smoke. Raheem closed the gate and was gone. Ayaan lit a cigar while walking around the compound.

It was a huge compound with a date palm tree in the corner. Yellow coloured ripe dates were hanging heavily in two bunches. Two girls, around twelve and ten years of age were playing with clay pots and sticks. In between the elder girl went to the date palm tree and tried to get some ripe dates with a palm stick. And it seemed almost impossible as she is too short to reach the bunch.

Ayaan approached them with a smile and asked. 'Can I help you?' Both of them were shy and left the palm tree and stood a little far away from him. He is a complete stranger for them.

He smiled again and asked them to come back. He said he can help them to get the dates. Finally they approached him slowly. Ayaan was tall enough to pluck the dates directly from the palm tree.

Shabaana and Nujoom were thrilled. They gratefully collected the dates from Ayaan.

Nabeesa and Alphy were inside the villa.

Alphy enquired her about the kids' school. Nabeesa's face went paler.

'We couldn't send our children to school because of

our illegal status. They don't even have their passports and birth certificates as three of them were delivered at home, except my elder daughter, Shabaana"

Alphy realised the horrifying situation of the family when she heard about the home delivery incident. They couldn't go out from their house even if they wished to. It was more or less like a prison.

Nabeesa is an English graduate, tutoring kids at home as they couldn't go to school without a valid visa. In fact, they had not realised on what they were missing out.

They lost everything in Umm al Quwain. Cheated by their sponsor, as he submitted Raheem's passport at the immigration department stating that his employee was absconding since one year.

It is their country. They can do as they please. Who will listen to us? How could we approach a police station or emigration department since we don't have our passport and visa.

My second delivery due date was getting close. I got my labour pain at midnight. That day Raheem's friend Khalid had come to inquire about our situation. He was like an angel sent to us from God. The same night, he took us all with our remaining belongings to his house in Fujairah.

I was screaming in pain when we reached Khalid's house. He was staying in a villa with bachelors. All of them were sleeping. He went and asked all of them to clear out, and made space for me to deliver my baby.

His neighbour, Khalid's friend's wife Saleema came to help. She turned to a mid-wife.

Nabeesa smiled at those terrible memories. The funniest part was that Saleema had married recently and pregnant with her first baby. Yet she gave me strength to push and stay calm during the most excruciating pain in the whole universe. That too, with her two month pregnancy.

I had delivered my second daughter, she was so small like a kitten, due to lack of nutrition and proper food.'

Nabeesa stopped in between when she saw Shabaana and Nujoom at the door. They were very happy holding a bunch of dates in their hands.

'Oh..ithu evidunnu kitti?' (Where did you get this from?)

Nabeesa asked in Malayalam.

Shabaana pointed to Ayaan who was entering the room.

He smiled at the kids and Nabeesa.

'Oh..did you say thank you to uncle ?'

'Yes , they did. They are very smart.' Ayaan complimented.

It was almost late afternoon. Nabeesa was looking outside the villa. She informed Ayaan and Alphy that Raheem might be late.

They said they would leave.

Nabeesa nodded. It seemed like she wanted to prepare something for kids. They must be hungry.

Alphy asked if she needed any help in the kitchen. She refused politely.

"Please come tomorrow morning itself. And you can have lunch with us." Nabeesa invited humbly.

They agreed. Children were waving at them happily when they closed the gate.

It's really strange to feel happy with people who were complete strangers till yesterday. She couldn't understand the significance of the pain while leaving them.

"What are the little girls' names?' Ayaan broke the silence.

'I didn't ask. What about the elder girls?'

"They are Shabaana and Nujoom. Alph, you won't

believe that the children were speaking English and Arabic very fluently. And they are really intelligent. They have left this house only twice in their entire life! Once to go to Ras Al Khaimah and the other time to Ajman. They haven't been to any other places in UAE"

Nabeesa and Raheem are graduates. Nabeesa has a diploma in basic computer applications. She is home schooling them. She teaches them in her own syllabus. Art, Music, Craft - everything combined.

"Shabaana sang for me. It's deadly. Blessed indeed!" Ayaan smiled.

"I think our conventional education system is pointless. Kids are sacrificing from their valuable time from childhood to youth to learn irrelevant, topics. When I was in school I hated history."

'Even I hate history!' Alphy whispered. After a moment she added, 'I hate math more!'

16

Alphy and Ayaan got into their car. It was parked near a Pakistani electrical and service workshop. There is a big tree filled with small leaves. A broken wooden ladder was propped up over the dirty wall of the shop. There were different types of refrigerators left open and covered in dust.

Alphy noticed a red fridge. It resembled a lady wearing only a red skirt, with her legs apart, worrying if an electrician will appear at any moment with his tools. She didn't know if he could fix her mechanical issues or if she would be dumped into scrap.

"All the shop shutters here are half the size of normal shutters. Did you notice that Alph?"

Ayaan voiced what she was also thinking. Alphy wondered, how could we think about the same topic at the same time?

Is there any dream analysing equipment invented somewhere in this universe?

Can't believe UAE has a hand in this situation. A rural and remote area where people are still living like Bedouins.

She was silent on their way back. Ayaan called Abdullah to his shop number and informed him that we had left Raheem's home little early and we could go back to visit the next morning.

Abdulla said that would be fine.

Ayaan asked if there is any good place for dinner. Abdullah suggested them to go to Coral beach Resort near Korfaqaan Cornish and if they are interested, there is a musical event also happening near to it. Ayaan asked her that they can go if she would be interested.Alphy was preoccupied thinking about those half ripe dates in those children's hands and their happiness in that moment.

Do they have enough food to eat?

"I really wish that idealistic travel document coined by Garry Davis would become a reality." Alphy sighed.

Ayaan hugged her with one hand while driving.

'It's your assignment ya habeebi! Don't get too empathetic.

" Seriously!! ? How could you be this insensitive Ayaan ? You heard all the horrible life threatening situations they have gone through! Still hiding through life..." Alphy was little devastated.

"Alph, Don't think of joining the Garry Davis club. The whole world is treating him like a lunatic you know."

What do you know about Garry Davis? Do you know that he was a pilot in the United States Army? He gave up his US citizenship after the grave shock and distress of bombing the city of Brandenburg in World War II. He saw the brutal deaths he had caused upon humanity!"

Alphy furiously diverted her gaze from Ayaan to the desert.

Ayaan stopped his BMW, in the emergency yellow lane of the highway and touched Alphy's shoulder.

"I am so sorry ya habeebi. I didn't mean to hurt you."

She looked at him.

" This is not the question of hurting me, instead you are humiliating a great human being who always wished for ONE WORLD with No war, No borders and territories.

He created a world passport, and he even travelled the world with that passport. Officials stopped him at the airports and ship ports, and was even sent to jail.

Still he continued his journey with the greatest

humanitarian message.

An international peace activist, that's what he is. If you feel he is as a freaking lunatic, then so Am I."

Ayaan started the vehicle and moved slowly, and quietly.

17

The next day, Alphy and Ayaan reached Raheem's place around eleven in the morning. They had bought some groceries, sweets, wafers and nuts for the children. Nabeesa and Raheem along with the kids welcomed them. Alphy felt like it was a family receiving their dear ones.

The son approached them and collected the grocery bags from them. Nabeesa shouted from behind,

"Aathif, you will fall..."

Alphy joyfully patted Aathif's cheek and took a

Snickers chocolate from the bag and gave it to him. Alphy had never seen a child with such huge eyes. He looked so innocent while carefully examining the chocolate over and over again.

On hearing his mother calling he ran away from them. He turned to look back at Alphy and Ayaan while he was running.

Alphy handed another chocolate to the third daughter, whose name she did not know yet. She took it with a grateful smile. Alphy patted her hair and asked her name.

'Zameena' she replied softly.

Raheem was asking why they took the trouble to bring so many things.

'It's for the kids. We have become friends since yesterday. Right girls?'

'Yes!'

Shabaana smiled at Ayaan and collected all the bags from them with her father's permission.

Alphy entered the house with Raheem's permission. Nujoom accompanied her to the kitchen where Nabeesa was busy preparing lunch for them.

The interior was old, with walls filled with cracks and dust. Nabeesa switched on the AC and it started with a windfall sound.

It was hot and humid inside!

Nabeesa was trying to make Alphy comfortable. Shabaana brought a wooden stool from inside.

"Please don't prepare anything extra for our sake. We just wanted to spend time with you and are happy to share what you have here. Don't go through any additional trouble for us!"

"Nothing much, Alphy. Whatever we can afford. That's all...

As a matter of fact, Raheem's friend, who helped us at Umm al Quwain during our tough times, is running a fish counter at the main fish market. Raheem also goes there to help him. Even though we are scared of the officers from the labor department who visits to conduct routine thaftheesh (inspection) for illegal employees. Other than that, we are able to earn a small amount as his share every day.

We just need food and very little clothing. No school fee, no medical expenses, not even a visit to the park or ice cream for the kids.'

Nabeesa's face was like a dimly light candle. Lit, but with shadows.

'Oh... labor inspection is also an issue here.' Alphy sighed anxiously.

'Yes. They check every two months and too unexpectedly! If they catch hold of him, they could put him in jail or even deport him. He is always worried about us! If they arrest him, at least he would be in jail here itself. But if they deport him, what would we do? Raheem cannot tell them that we are here as long as we are illegal immigrants. We will all have to go to jail then, know?”

Alphy felt terrified thinking about the families trapped in this dangerous situation.

It was a delicious Kerala Meal! Alphy was familiar with the taste. She had tried all sorts of food as she has friends from various states back in India.

Journalist Academy Bangalore is one of the best colleges for journalism and mass communication studies. They provide exemplary training. Therefore most of the smart, daring, hot-blooded students apply and compete to get into JAB.

But she had never tasted such delectable Kerala cuisine since she had left Bangalore for Dubai. It has been almost a year. It was a completely new taste for Ayaan.

Raheem courteously asked whether they were okay with the food or they can make chapatti.

‘No, it is absolutely fine and delicious!’

Ayaan answered earnestly and Alphy could see that he was being truthful as she saw the way he was enjoying the food!

18

There are three cats inside the compound. Two of them are white with black patches and the third one is grey in colour. The kids were feeding them leftovers. Little Asker was looking at them with a gloomy face. He thinks the kitten needs milk but his mom won't allow him to feed them milk from his glass.

Ayaan was curious. He was wondering how they will feed the cats when they are short of food for themselves.

Nabeesa was explaining about the time when Nujoom fell sick with pneumonia and how desperately she wailed praying to God, in the middle of the desert during a night of rain and thunder! Nujoom suffered with heavy blotted lungs and she arched back like an arrow gasping for a mouthful of air!

Delivery of Asker was by far the most tragic one. It was taken by Raheem alone. They didn't even notice she was pregnant until she reached seven months! She had no belly at all!! Moreover missed or delayed menstrual cycle was a usual thing for Nabeesa.

Alphy heard her voice breaking while talking. She paused in between. They could hear the birds chirping. The tiny yellow bird started flying faster. She noticed that the cage occupies a lot of space in their small dining room.

When they bid farewell, it was late evening that day. Alphy could see the hope in their eyes. It was shining with the anticipation of freedom! They wanted to be beside their parents in their old age. Children could finally meet their grandparents. At least they should know and realise that there is a world out there filled with people and possibilities!

Ayaan asked Raheem for both of their passport copies. It was an old photocopy showing that the passport had expired five years back. Raheem's passport might be withheld at Umm Al Quwain immigration department.

'Do we also get new passports?'

Shabaana asked Alphy while they were walking to the gate.

Alphy couldn't answer. The little girl was waiting for her to respond.

Ayaan saw a teardrop in Alphy's eyes. He replied 'Yes' to Shabaana and patted her head.

She was ecstatic! Alphy could see a globe dissolving into her eyes with joy.

Alphy listened to her queries. She wanted to know how her school would be and how many friends she would make there.

Alphy followed Ayaan who was walking ahead of her. She noticed a pearl white Mazda 323 car with no number plate. It was parked in Raheem's backyard , and was full of scratches and dents. Desert dust storms had blanketed the car. Abdulla said it was Raheem's car and he couldn't renew it after he lost his passport and visa documents. He couldn't even resell it as it didn't have a renewed Mulkiya (registration) .

It was a brand new car that he had purchased with a bank loan. Unfortunately he couldn't even use it for a year!

Ayaan and Alphy thanked Abdullah. Ayaan shook his hand and they greeted each other on parting.

'Brother Ayaan and sister Alphy... if you can do anything to help these poor, helpless family, please do it! May Allah give you thaakath(strength) for that.

Assalamu alaikum.'

Ayaan agreed to do their best.

'Va aalikumussalaam ya rafeeq... insha allah. mahassalaamah.

'Mahassalaama.'

They hugged each other.

Abdullah said good bye to Alphy and she greeted him back with a feeble voice.

She couldn't speak a word with Ayaan on their way back to their villa. She felt disgusted with him. Alphy couldn't understand the logic of his promise to Raheem's family.

Contrarily her assignment may bring them in front of the law and they might go to jail forever.

She decided to forget about the screening assignment for Connector magazine and didn't even bother about the missed calls from her Managing Director, Amith Gautham.

19

"What happened habeebi?"

Ayaan noticed the way Alphy was laying on the bed. It meant she wanted him to know that she has no interest, not even to talk.

Ayaan removed his sleeveless vest and hugged her tightly from behind. Alphy liked that posture. She loved his deep, passionate kisses on her shoulder and bare neck. She loved the way he savoured her taste buds. She went wild when he inhaled the scent of her underarms. She always wanted to invent something to make him astounded and overwhelmed.

Ayaan always teased her after they invent each other on the bed.

"Are there more floods for me to gulp dear...? More islands to be revealed ?"

Alphy tried to explain those feelings several times. But feelings don't possess a language. In other words, only a body can sense and understand what exactly the other craves! When you kiss your lady, she returns it multifold! Hug her and she squeezes you, like the way we squeeze the pulp to get the last drop of juice!

The following morning, Ayaan asked her to pack her things immediately. She was still in bed. She hadn't slept properly as the children's innocent faces kept popping her awake.

'Why suddenly?'

'Mukthar wants me back before noon. Got an emergency at office.'

Alphy checked her mobile screen and saw that the

time was 8'o clock. Ayaan had taken a bath already. Alphy got ready within an hour. They had a club sandwich and orange juice .

Mukthar's Nigerian cook was a bit disappointed as all the special dishes he had prepared for them had gone to waste.

"Please don't mind my friend... I have to reach my office immediately! Your arabab is my arabab also, and he asked me to do so."

Ayaan smiled at him and gave him and the Filipino house keeper 100 dirhams each. They were very happy and asked Alphy to come visit again as she was saying goodbye to them.

On the way Ayaan was unusually silent and concentrating on the road in front of them. Alphy didn't ask why. She was thinking about the invisible wall between them, even though they right next to each other.

The wall was always there. She sensed it right from the moment they met. But never questioned Ayaan about it. She was observing him when he was silent. She felt that even though his surface was still, the undercurrent must be gushing!

She was not sure whether to question him about what was on his mind or not to disturb his thoughts.

She decided to remain quiet as it would hurt her if he did not respond.

At times, she wanted to open up about the invisible wall. He might tease her. And he would definitely say that an architect would not understand the creative madness and fantasies of an artist.

She paints. People close to her knows that. She is not interested in exhibiting it. She considers it as her private strokes and doesn't want to share it with the outside world.

Bob is a good viewer and always enjoys her work.

Bob falls in her wavelength and he admires her poetic sense unconventionally. He speaks very little about it, but from a terrific critic like him, few words are worth enough.

20

Ayaan went to Lebanon.

Alphy didn't feel any sadness about the unexpected return journey. She was used to it and didn't think too much about the commitments or ethics of people in love when it comes to Ayaan.

She intentionally doesn't try to solve the puzzle. She was scared of discovering the truth about love and its divinity. She wasn't even sure if something of that kind exists. You could say parting ways with Ayaan terrified her. She believed that the invisible wall would vanish, as she waited for something miraculous, like the illuminati would shine a ray of enlightenment on the intensity and core of their bond!

Thoughts are like unexpected thunder. We are frightened by its reverberation and , vulnerable when it crashes out of the blue. No one desires repulsive thoughts!

We humans blame 'the devil; whenever things go out of hand. We say that the devil has only one job in the universe. Manipulate the thoughts of human beings, make them frustrated or depressed, and gain an upper hand forever...'

Alphy never agreed to this notion. She believes God and Devil lives inside each of us. When we intently observe our thoughts at least a week , you can easily identify the good and bad that is happening around us driven by our positive and negative thoughts.

No matter how hard you try to control your mind, you can resist only for a short while. Our mind is well aware that thoughts define our destiny. It knows that positive thoughts will pilot us to live in the present. It knows that we will contemplate our past, connect the dots and move forward with confidence! But the mind doesn't want that. It is, terrified of losing control over a human. Mankind never realises the potential of their consciousness.

The devil is a punctilious soul who never runs away from his duty. He is enslaved within his past. Men forgive him at times but he forgets that he had been forgiven.

'Ayaan is a good soul. He would never hurt Alphy'.

Alphy meditated and whispered to her soul every morning. That is what brahmayoga preaches. She likes to listen to B K Shivani, even though she is sceptical on her views about karma, she still watches her talks on YouTube.

And she realises that how much ever she tries to move away from him, it is just not possible! She doesn't believe in soul mates, but she believes in pain. She couldn't believe in love without pain. If God is the synonym of love... then why should we suffer for love!

Ayaan hadn't called since they parted after their journey to Fujairah. Alphy's thoughts tried to comfort her.

But she still checked her mobile every morning, afternoon, evening and sometimes in the middle of the night.

She consoled herself saying it will be okay. But she couldn't quite make out the real source of the pain pricking her uncomfortably.

The heart has many chambers. Biologically it may have four, but intuitionally it has plenty. On occasion, it beats quickly and horribly furious, like a reckless motorbike.

21

Alphy was acclimatising at Connector. Amith Gautham is a nice man. He reminded her only once about the screening assignment's status.

Gautham was very punctual in their office proceedings and his interaction with colleagues. They had a monthly get-together at different hotels. He knew the pulse of a journalist and how to make him productive and beneficial for the media world.

Never expect criticism from Amith. He won't utter a word about your story if it's not worthwhile. He doesn't give you a second chance to re-write it or do a fresh piece on the same topic.

According to Amith Gautham, time is the heart of media. If you waste a minute, you will skip a milestone from your career.

The screening assignment for new recruitment was Amith's new strategy to judge the caliber of the recruit. He started that process at connector. Amith Gautham is well aware of the environment of the media world in Arab countries.

He never compromises with the schedule. Six months probation with an interesting assignment to be fulfilled; If not, quit the job.

At one of the monthly get-together, held at Dubai Golf and Yacht Club, a boat-shaped five star hotel, with spreading golf lawns, Amith invited Alphy to dance with him.

Even though she wasn't in the mood to dance, she didn't want to offend him. She kept her wine glass on the table and accompanied Amith to the dance floor.

Amith was holding Alphy and moving to the music of Christina Perri's 'A Thousand years'

'I have loved you for a thousand years , I'll love you for a thousand more ...

I will not let anything take away,

What's standing in front of me...'

Alphy suddenly lost her balance and fainted. Amith got a hold of her and everyone gathered around

Alphy who was unconscious in Amith Gautham's lap.

Bob and Sheaba were seated beside Alphy's bed at American Hospital.

Alphy was taken to the hospital by Amith and a few colleagues from the party. Bob and Sheaba reached the hospital immediately. She was still under observation at that time. The office staff left after they reached and Amith asked Bob to call in case of any emergency.

Alphy opened her eyes and smiled at Sheaba and Bob. Alphy hold on to worried Sheaba's hand.

Their expression was one that Alphy was not familiar with. She couldn't exactly recall what happened at the party.

I drank only a glass of wine and then came Amith's invitation to dance. And then...

Did I see Ayaan there?

Alphy couldn't clear the fog from her memories.

Yes, I saw him. While I was dancing to 'A thousand years.'

It's been three weeks since he left for Lebanon and not even a message had been sent.

Alphy felt like it's been a thousand years, and she cried like a helpless child who was standing abandoned on a cliff.

22

"Bob,it's been a week. Alphy extended her leave for three more days. Something is brewing inside her..."

Sheaba was waiting for an answer from Bob. But he didn't reply instantly.

He was thinking about Sheaba's uncertainty. Something is going on with Alphy. Even he felt so. But he never wanted to ask and interfere if she was trying to solve it herself. Self healing is the best medicine for a peaceful soul. Alphy is a sturdy , self-composed lady.

Shaeba loved her deeply. She used to tell Bob that she wanted to marry Alphy when they were in college together. She wanted to hold her hand wherever they went. She liked to smell her hair. She wanted to lean on her shoulders when they were in the canteen during their coffee break.

Alphy loved her too. In fact Shaeba's passionate love made her hold on to their friendship. Alphy always kept a bewildering personal space. A duel personality, like a two-sided coin, but in a sense of strength and maturity.

One face had a drive to look at things in a logical and practical way. People who were encircled there have taken her valuable opinion in their life decisions. The other face is highly sensitive, passionate, love seeking and unable to progress without emotional bonding.

She is patient , humble and has her own charisma. People often misunderstood her nature as big-headed.

Shaeba knew that it was just a mask. Alphy's mother, Christina aunty, struggled a lot to raise her. She felt very lonely when her mom was travelling and got engaged with work at her event management company in Bangalore. She started as a low key venture organising small marriages and other private events. Later she flourished to be a high profile wedding planner creating numerous stellar events! She was a hardcore workaholic throughout her life. She struggled a lot with Alphy's adolescent ecstasies.

Alphy loved her mom profoundly and missed her presence through every stage of her life. Long since, she accepted the reality of loneliness. She reserved herself into the apartment.

She paints well. Her bedroom was a metamorphosis of her artistic talent. The walls change colour and pattern time and again. Shaeba was the only visitor allowed to enter her room.

Alphy kept a beautiful distance with her mom. They loved each other like no one has before. Yet, they couldn't figure out the serenity between their loves.

The constant longing for her mom during her childhood had shattered her. She was vibrant, or did she have an extrovert mask very firmly fitted for her close ones to see?

Shaeba never complained about Alphy's uncanny behaviour. She loved her with all her eccentricities. Bob consumes Alphy silently, they have developed a full-grown acquaintance,which is very divergent from Shaeba.

Acceptance of habits will make you comfortable with anyone. Even if he is an offender, you could easily accept the prototype of his wrong doings.

Self destruction is the worst opponent of human beings. Knowing one's limitations, yet still unwilling to accept it, is the pitiable stage.

Shaeba always prayed for Alphy. She knew how much the girl had suffered with her depression and dual personality, even though she has a mastermind.

Alphy posses an extra sensory perception, which usually ends up to be true most of the time. She could especially sense danger that was waiting to unfold.

She was well aware of her dear ones' need and she would do anything to make it happen.

23

Alphy grew close with a boy during their college days. He was a crazy guy. But Alphy was his most trusted friend. Sheaba warned Alphy not to blindly trust him, but Alphy used to say that she trusted her own intuition when it came to understanding people.

Abhinav mailed a love letter to Alphy. We were all amused to hear the news and teased him. Alphy didn't get upset with him. She asked him to meet her at the backyard of the college ground. He was anxious wondering if she wanted to scold him. The ground was muddy due to heavy rain the previous night. Huge banyan trees were guarding the ground, the long tentacles touching the mud and the leaves were falling even in the gentle breeze. The banyan tree resembled a gigantic witch who had spun her hair as a web to catch prey. But the prey loved it. They were the erotic lovers in their teens, who longed to touch and caress each other.

No one was comfortable with him except Alphy, during our gruelling internship phase. Alphy gladly chose him as her intern partner.

Sheaba got really worried whenever she was late to return from her assignments. Abhi always preferred to travel on his bullet. He had a black coloured thunderbird. He used to speed up to 80 and it flied like a phoenix! Alphy wasn't frightened at all.

Abhi dropped out of the college and never returned. Even Alphy's ESP didn't see it coming and it shattered everyone, especially Alphy.

It was a grave shock for the gang. Sheaba had no clue to date about why Alphy had asked Abhi to meet her at the backyard of the banyan tree. She never asked Alphy. The truth was that even Alphy didn't know Abinav's whereabouts. A Delhi based millionaire's son. In faculty's eye, a spoiled brat!

Alphy shut herself inside her room for more than two weeks. She didn't speak to anybody including her mom. She opened the door for me and I went and sat near the balcony window in silence. I sat there for hours and returned with unspoken words. That was the most hard and painful time for Sheaba.

She was scared that Alphy would go back into that closed room syndrome again. And she still didn't know how to tackle the situation if it happened again.

24

"Bob, I think I' m not feeling well..."

Alphy came out of her room on the fifth day after the hospital incident and sat on Sheaba and Bob's living room couch.

Bob looked at Alphy calmly. Sheaba didn't say a word though she was feeling worried and anxious.

Bob was waiting for Alphy's next sentence.

There was a long silence then. Alphy slowly started

"I don't know...

Ayaan left for Lebanon the same day we reached back from Fujairah."

Bob and Sheaba were listening.

"I don't know, I was fine with the way he disappears. I could handle these situations. I know I can't do anything much about this behaviour... as a matter of fact, that's not him behaving. That's his bad mood acting up. We should be mindful that a person is never born with any negative qualities or habits. It is the situation and surrounding that influences them. Family, friends circle, where he was brought up, what kind of schooling...etc. He is a residential school product you know..."

Bob didn't say a word. He knew well about Alphy's State of mind when it comes to Ayaan. She will defend him with her full heart. Bob knew that the girl is defending it out of her innocent love for love for him. And that was the problem.

Sheaba was growing more anxious and she was

furious with the Lebanese fellow who was constantly stressing her best friend. She used to refer to Ayaan as 'Lebanee...'

"But he is not the same man now. Believe me Bob, I can see the judgement in your eyes. At least, now he is answering my calls or responding to my messages. He changed a lot in a positive way recently.»

Bob felt that Alphy was trying to console herself more than trying to convince them. He didn't want to offend her.

"Something does not feel right though..." Alphy lowered her voice.

"What happened?" Bob asked

"I tried his Lebanon number many times. He said he will be back after two or three days. It's been more than three weeks now, and there is no news from him."

"But, you know how he is. And you are supposed to be okay with it. Right?»

«It's not okay now. I can't be okay. Truth be told, I have never been okay. Love is such a crazy rollercoaster! Bob, Once you get into it, and if your heart desires it, you won't be able to get down. You think you are trying with all your effort, but you're mistaken. You cannot try wholeheartedly. Your mind traps you, no matter how hard you try.»

"No dear, please don't glorify that lebanee now. He has given you enough." Shaeba responded little louder involuntarily.

Alphy grew silent.

She started to look out through the balcony. Sheikh Zayed Road was packed with evening traffic. People are walking on the pavement in front of Holiday Inn hotel, hustling back and forth from work. Most of them were in a hurry to be someplace. There were a few chattering with their friends and moving ahead collectedly. Some of them were on their phone.

Did everyone have someone to talk to? Are they happy? Or are their faces troubled by pain? Who is able to hear their palpitation audibly?

Alphy's thoughts were wandering like a stray dog.

Bob and Sheaba were waiting for her to come back.

"I'm pregnant."

Alphy breaks the silence.

25

Ayaan called exactly twenty-three days; after he left. He sounded relentless.

Alphy could hear her own voice. Was it slightly wavering?

Alphy was picturing Ayaan's face when he hears the good news!

She really longed to witness the moment.

Alphy couldn't figure out if the news was good or bad yet. She couldn't contemplate the consequences. She deliberately shut out thoughts of the reactions of her mom, her elite social relations, clients and their other relatives back home.

To what extent an unmarried lady could consider it as 'good news'?

Alphy was flustered when she missed her cycle. There was no possibility of conceiving during their time together at Fujairah. It was just seven days after her cycle. Alphy calculated that it fell into the safe period.

Her gynaecologist informed her that there is no such period. No day is safe if you are not planning to conceive.

"Did you use any protection?"

"No, we don't usually use any protection"

"Then how can you be so certain that you wouldn't conceive?"

"It worked perfectly fine all these years. We've been together for more than four years now. Our time together was always unpredictable and unplanned."

‘How old are you?’

"Thirty four"

“’And your partner?’

"Thirty-six"

“So... both of you are not underage. You are educated enough to know the repercussions of unprotected sex.»

Alphy kept quiet.

It was not just sex. She cannot reveal the divinity and wildness of their love. She couldn't explain to the doctor that sex always happened between them organically. It blossomed naturally!

«It happens through its own construct. And we didn’t bother about the shield or protection from the wholeness. Are we the only ones who feel this way or do all couples echo the same sentiment? The answer is irrelevant. No two emotional connections would ever be the same!

We don’t even know when is the ideal time. Is there a right moment to move away and find some cover to protect their love when it's at its peak?»

The doctor smiled at her,

“Alphy, I like the spirit of your love.Love has no rules. But as long as we are staying in a different country we are compelled to obey their rules. Isn’t it so?”

Alphy didn't reply. She didn’t agree that a country has anything to do interfering their love either.

“You have to register your marriage as early as possible. You can do your regular check-ups , follow-ups and delivery only if you are legally married here”

26

Ayaan lost his cool and got upset when Alphy broke the news.

He was blaming her stating that she did not take care of the protection. He implied that women should be responsible for it.

Alphy felt her choking after a while now. It was not the usual palpitation when Ayaan disappears without a heads up. It was much louder. Loud enough that she could hear the scream of an unborn child.

She recalled the whispers of their private moments, him begging her for a baby.

She never thought of using a baby to get him forever nor to poison his life.

It was the blame, the humiliation and every accusation thrown at her...

She vomited appallingly.

27

Ayaan said he was only concerned about his five year old daughter back in Lebanon. His wife had filed for divorce and demanded for alimony to fix the wound inflicted as his wife.

28

It was another blow for Alphy. Bob asked her to save the baby and not to think too much about Ayaan.

Easier said than done. Alphy withdrew from the world like never before.

She was lying on her bed. She pressed her palms against the right side of her stomach. She could feel the breathing. She remembered the doctor's words.

"Please get legally married as early as possible.'

Ayaan was endlessly sending messages from Lebanon.

"Never bring a child without identity into this world. Don't punish me and my daughter. I never expected you to go to this extent. It's so cheap! Almighty will punish you!"

Alphy's mind was blank.

She couldn't figure out what exactly was happening in her life. She wanted to disappear. Ayaan was acting like a complete stranger throwing reckless words at her. She was trying to forget.

It was him always going on about their baby and their life together. He wanted a baby with her face. He even begged her to take a year off to have a baby.

Alphy tried to explain calmly about the consequences then. She was worried about her mom and that she may not agree to their relationship. Without her mom's consent, Alphy won't be able to take a decision.

Ayaan always considered it as an excuse. He was convinced that their different religions was what mattered to her. Maybe not as much to her; but for her mom. And the differences went beyond that, it was trans-national.

She was thinking about the invisible wall.

Alphy couldn't decipher her mind when she thinks about a life with Ayaan. She was completely in love with him, and shared joy with utmost purity.

During her college days she never broke her boundary of values. The definition of values was also up for question. Her values may differ from others.

She was always surrounded by teenagers who believed that love was just a tool to enjoy life. They were exploring their youth and used to compare which is the sweetest they had tasted so far. Most of the girls had a 'why should girls suppress all the fun' attitude.

The students, for money and materialistic gain, turned lovers for business tycoons. They accompanied playing the role of a secretary or mistress. They relished the most expensive liquor at the most luxurious hotel suites with their temporary boss and got well paid before their flight back to Bangalore.

Alphy can try to understand if girls from poorer backgrounds will be willing to do all this for money. It's justifiable if they desire worldly luxury, which they have never experienced before.

But girls from well off families were more in number. Was it for their sexual ecstasy? Alphy never understood their justification. Let them enjoy the pleasure, but why take money? She was not okay with those who were ready to take off their clothes just to have momentary fun in their life. Alphy was not a person with reserved ideology. She didn't believe she would have sex after marriage if there was no love. She didn't believe solely in simple desire!

Love can connect two souls. She didn't believe in marriage if there is no love. She didn't believe in compromise only to live up to the expectations of society.

She won't place her beautiful body in altar, if it did not musically fulfil the divinity of two souls. She believed that souls have to be loved unconditionally.

She always disagreed with Bob.

He says that,

"Love cannot be everlastingly unconditional. There are commitments. If there is no commitment, it's just a tool to fill the devil's pot"

When you are in love, it hurts at time. But it cannot be pain for three hundred days in a year. When you are with someone, to whom you surrender both your blood and soul, he should respect your love. He shouldn't abandon his girl in a vacuum.

He still hasn't realised the value of your heart

Alphy... He considers you according to his convenience.

And you are happily accepting that under the illusion that the man still loves you.

He doesn't deserve you Alphy. Please grow up!"

29

Alphy couldn't sleep at night. She heard a cry most of the time in her sleep. She saw Ayaan holding a sword saying, "Kill it ya habeebi. Kill it."

Alphy wanted to take up the role of a hang women in her life. She saw a hanging tree in her dreams.

Bob came to her solace whenever he was at home.

"Don't worry too much about him, he is already a devil wanting to kill the baby."

"But Bob.. It's not about him, it's about his daughter in Lebanon." Alphy murmured.

"Yes. For him, it's about his daughter . What about your baby? You don't even know if it's a boy or girl. You don't even know the colour and features of the baby; he or she might look like you.

It's a life growing inside you Alphy. Nothing justifies your first option."

The first option was abortion as Ayaan suggested. Shaeba also wanted her to abort the baby. She was angry like a provoked angel. Even if she disagreed with the lebanee, she believed in Alphy and her faith in him.

She believed in Alphy and her faith like ten commandments. She was under the impression that Ayaan will do anything to be with her. Shaeba was secretly jealous that Ayaan was the luckiest man in the world to have her best friend's love and trust.

More than anybody, Shaeba was well aware of Alphy's intense love towards Ayaan.

She thought Ayaan also knew that. No matter;

whatever stupid habits he posses. No matter how selfish he was at that time.

Sheaba couldn't control her distress. She blasted out.

Alphy decided to go ahead with the second option as Bob had said.

Go back to Bangalore and deliver her baby there and return after that. Alphy finally settled on her decision. She thought she could even convince her mom. She even had a false marriage story planned.

"Then what ?" Shaeba was fuming.

She fought with Bob and he kept quiet. Bob asked Alphy to go to church and surrender to the cross. He said Jesus will guide her to the truth.

Alphy gathered strength in Bob's words. She saw infant Jesus in Mother Mary's hands. She saw her, insulted and humiliated by the people of Jerusalem, cursed as a whore. Date palm trees bowed to provide her shade and gave her dates when she was hungry. She stumbled upon a stream in the desert when she was thirsty.

Cows and calves surrounded her in the stable when she got her labor pain.

It was dark. A shooting star shone light to the sky!

Jesus was Born!

30

Alphy was sitting silently in her room at Bangalore. Her mom couldn't figure out her daughter's emergency visit.

She didn't question her. But she could sense that something was off and her eyes were pale and bloodless. Christina couldn't budge from her seat and she couldn't speak for long, neither could Alphy. Alphy couldn't lie to her mom.

Alphy was looking outside her window. She saw that black fumes were rising from the streets high into the air. There was pollution everywhere. Air, water, vegetables, fruits, meat, fish. Everything was contaminated with pesticides.

It was poisonous food and water we were taking in. Poisonous oxygen we were exhaling.

Alphy could see her face in everything. It was natural to be poisonous.

She smiled to herself.

Am I poisonous? Then how am I supposed to deliver my baby unharmed into this poisonous world?

Alphy noticed a homeless lady on the street sitting near the road barricade. She was trying to pick up something from the ground. What was it? Alphy couldn't see it clearly as her balcony window curtains were swaying in the light breeze, obscuring her vision.

It is mostly hot during the day in Bangalore, but cold at times.

Alphy asked if her mom could slightly move away

from the balcony window so that she could see what exactly the lady was trying to pick up. Christina stared back at her. Alphy felt her mom's eyes grow more pale.

The lady was picking up leftover food from a plastic bag. Somebody had dumped their waste on the street. Night was the cloak to litter. Those who wanted to litter their frustrations will be awake and wandering.

Dubai creeped into Alphy's thoughts. One of the cleanest cities. If the men wear any other colour of kandhura, other than the purest white, wouldn't it be odd. People are not only considering their own health, but also other human beings in their periphery. They want the next generation to live their life in a clean city.

Then why are people are still selfish?

They carelessly throw waste away from their compound to make their lives neat and comfortable. They are planting fresh vegetables for their own children and see other children as commodity.

They take long baths with bath salts until they feel relaxed and don't even bother to drain the used water into the waste pit?

"He's not a real man."

Christina was pouring coffee into Alphy's mug. It was the second day after Alphy reached Bangalore. Her mom didn't say a word for the last two days. Alphy didn't seem to notice. She was in a dilemma of whether to take the folic acid tablets or not. The gynaecologist from Dubai gave her the tablets when the pregnancy was initially confirmed. She held her positive test results in her hand by that time.

After all the discussions that Alphy had with the doctor, she advised her to continue the pregnancy. And for a healthy baby, the mother has to be healthy.

Alphy couldn't even believe what she had just

heard. It took more than an hour to come back to reality.

Doctor advised her to take folic acid tablets regularly and stay healthy to ensure delivery of a healthy baby.

She even started taking the tablets from next day onwards. She didn't even know what was to come. She didn't get Ayaan on the phone. She didn't even think about how we should handle the situation. But she knew that Ayaan will be happy to hear the news. It is definitely a good news for him since he's been waiting for this from the moment we met.

She laughed out loud.

Christina shook Alphy's shoulder. Her mom was frightened by her expression.

Alphy declined the coffee. "It's not good for baby you know. We cannot take caffeine products mama, it's very bad for the baby."

Christina hugged her tightly and cried.

Alphy was shocked to see her crying. Before the pregnancy, she had never seen more than two drops of tears in her mama's eyes.

"Alphy ...did you hear what mama said?"

"No."

"If he was a real man, he wouldn't have escaped from this situation. He blamed you and cleared his side. He may be a good father or son. But he won't be a good partner."

This was the first time Alphy kept quiet when she heard someone criticise Ayaan. She was thinking about all those arguments at Bob's place. She never listened to anyone who blamed him. Not even her best friend Sheaba. Alphy trusted him blindly. She didn't care how bad he ignores her and disappears. She cried a lot. She couldn't breathe. Still she was trying to find justification for his deeds.

She deliberately tried to move away from him. It

was just not possible when you are deeply in love. It doesn't matter how your partner feels. Did he love you the way you love him, care for you the way you care for him. Did he miss you the way you miss him night after night?

"It is the difference between men and women habeebi. I love you! I don't know if I do as much as you. But I do know that it's growing day by day."

Alphy closed her ears with her hands to restrain his sound entering furiously and screamed on her mama's shoulder.

31

Dr. Babitha Rao owned one of the best super specialty hospitals in Bangalore. She is mama's soul mate. They share everything. Alphy knows Babitha Aunty since her first memories.

Dr Babitha was stunned looking at Alphy. Babitha Aunty is the smartest in their group.

"Oh, you've grown so pretty! Are you really coming from Dubai? You must see when people come back from gulf! More fair, slight chubbiness and naturally flushed cheeks..."

Alphy smiled knowingly. She knew Babita Aunty would notice her changes better than her mom.

Alphy knows she is trying to cheer her up. Mom would have told her the whole story.

"Babitha aunty, could you be honest with me ? I have a question."

"Yes, dear... always. Go ahead."

"I had my ultra sound scan done at Dubai, and the doctor said that the baby's heart has started to beat. Is this true?

Dr Babitha had gone through all her reports and had finished scrutinising each and every point.

"Not really Alph... it's only been six weeks. Heartbeats only start after at least eight weeks."

" But the doctor said... she even showed me the position of the heart on the screen"

Dr. Babitha patted Alphy's shoulder.

" That must have been fetal movements of some sort which was misinterpreted. Most of the medical practitioners are not well experienced in gulf countries. That's a major issue there. Even though technology is at its peak, with all the world wonders and constant inventions...

But when it comes to medical issues and the situation is critical, even the Arab nationals are approaching India or US; right?

You must already know all this, my young, pretty, daring journalist"

Dr. Babitha laughed again. Alphy's mom also joined. Alphy could see; they were trying to cool down the situation.

"But the nervous system forms by the fourth week right? Including brain cells, heart muscles?"

Christina kept silent. Her eyes were brimming again.

"Look at me Alph. Don't go web surfing too much, it won't be as accurate as you think."

" I am a science graduate, Babitha Aunty. Your son was my class mate. Have you forgotten that or trying to calm me down?"

It's fine... The decision is not for me now. Everything is for a five year old girl in Lebanon. And I want to let my baby go without choking in my womb... I don't want to hear the cry. "

Alphy was directed to the nurses' station. A head nurse accompanied her at the special request of Dr. Babitha. The nurse gave her an oval shaped tablet to insert into her vagina. She instructed Alphy to insert it at night whenever she feels fine and comfortable.

Alphy didn't agree. She asked the nurse to do it on the spot, as she was scared that after she leaves from the hospital she might change her mind again. She was scared with a delay of even a day, and the baby might start breathing.

34

Bangalore was cold the very same night.

Alphy felt like her heart was broken into pieces and bleeding, when she saw the first spot of blood on her panty lining. She stared at the spot. It was not just a blood stain. It was her baby's blood.

She touched it and cried more loudly.

It was a Monday.

The air was broiling when Alphy was admitted at the hospital. Alphy heard her mom weeping and requesting Babitha aunty that her daughter wouldn't suffer even the slightest pain.

"She'll feel nothing Christina. She will be completely under anaesthesia. It's just a half an hour procedure only."

Alphy smiled again.

Alphy was at the operation table . There were nurses and an anaesthetist along with

Dr Babitha.

Babitha aunty came close to Alphy. Alphy didn't smile. She wanted to say something to Babitha aunty. She wanted to ask her to take the baby out gently. She didn't want to hurt her baby.

Dr Babitha introduced Alphy to others.

"She is a famous journalist, internationally renowned! She covered the Iraq – Iran interior riots and was accredited by government."

Everyone looked up at Alphy with adoration. The anaesthetist shook her hand and said that he had read the news and it was indeed a brave attempt in her journalism career.

He raised the syringe and smiled at her.

"Don't worry, it is just a small doze. You won't feel any pain," the doctor added.

Alphy closed her eyes. Daring journalist, Proud reporter...

Alphy transformed into a worm following the pricking pain of the needle on her arm.

A worm that slithers in the mud, which cannot even comprehend if there is a definition for life and death.

35

Alphy was coiled up on the single-seater couch when her mother entered the living room. It had been three days since the hospital episode. Her mother didn't go for work for the first time in her life. Alphy was smiling at her. Christina was shocked to see her daughter lying like a centipede, shrivelling on the couch. There was a three-seater sofa in the centre of the room with two single-seaters on either side. It was made of pine wood and covered in rich, olive-green fabric.

Christina sometimes slept on the three-seater couch comfortably, whenever she reached home late at night from events, without even changing her clothes. But being cramped up into the single sofa was an uncomfortable sight.

Alphy didn't look up at Christina's face. Her eyes weren't closed either.

She felt like someone had stranded her in the desert after amputating her without her consent. What is the most important organ for a human being?

Lungs? Heart? Eyes? Brain?

She laughed unexpectedly at her last option. It was most definitely not the brain.

Why was the human created with both brain and heart? The brain didn't get along with the heart. Heart's chambers are constantly pumping emotions at every heartbeat. There are millions of emotions wandering in search of their real identity.

Humans didn't even understand why all these feelings were germinating every second. Anger, hatred, passion, jealousy, ego, love... Which is the outstanding one?

Is it Pain?

Don't all these emotions ultimately end up in pain?

Love is an amalgamation.

Alphy asked her mom to sit beside her. Christina sat next to her and held Alphy's hand like a baby.

"Mama...

Love is the only emotion that is composed of both pleasure and pain."

Her daughter was the strongest girl she ever came across and she was always proud of her. She never questioned any of her decisions from a very early age. She never felt any need for it. Alphy was quite capable in her capacity to do so; her schooling, her journalism path, her job at Bangalore.

Christina felt a little dejected when Alphy told her about the Dubai job offer. She didn't object, but for the first time in her life, she felt that she was going to be alone.

Christina was busy throughout her life. She wanted to give her daughter everything that she wanted after her father left this world. She neither wanted to depend on her husband's family nor hers. Her parents asked her to re-marry when Alphy was five years old. A proposal from Canada was almost fixed. Her parents promised her that they will take care of Alphy, even more than they had taken care of Christina, and she could peacefully live her life in Canada with her partner.

Christina laughed when she thought of 'peace without her daughter.' It was she who decided to fight for her life independently.

Alphy rested her head in Christina's lap.

"Mama... You left me alone during my childhood. Why did you leave me all alone? I was scared most of the time as a child. You didn't even have time to read me a bedtime story. Yes, Aunt Reenu was there with me, trying to replace your presence. That's what she had been telling me all those years. She kept reminding me, 'I'm there for you, in place of your mama."

But the void was left hollow, especially when she kept reminding me every day. I heard those words even in my dreams at night. Alphy laughed out loud.

I loved her. But she was never you. No one can replace a mother's position. Isn't it?"

Alphy paused.

"I wouldn't have done that mama. I shouldn't have..."

"Guddiyaa..please stay calm. It's in the past now."

"It's in the past because I made it so. He or she could have still been inside my stomach;growing day by day;breathing, kicking, and pushing against me. I could have delivered my baby after nine months ma...

I committed a crime. I should surrender to the police. I need to be punished. Don't you think so? Hang till death."

Christina was horrified to watch Alphy crawling like a centipede again.

Her mother couldn't say a word. She went into her room and tried Dr. Babitha, but it was continuously engaged. Another call crept in-between. Christina answered. It was Sheaba.

"Aunty, Alphy is not answering her phone.

Is everything okay there?"

Christina kept quiet.

Alphy was sitting for a while now, in the bathtub filled with hot water. She spent most of her time in the bathtub now. She was still bleeding. She felt her bed will be drenched in blood. She had been changing napkins every half an hour, which later reduced fifteen-minute intervals. She had been thinking about Ayaan, both when she slept or was awake. She couldn't forget his harsh words.

She has been trying to ascertain her mistake. Whenever she tries to solve the puzzle, she bleeds more.

She was tired of changing napkins. Aunt Reenu was with her most of the time, even though they didn't talk much. Christina and Aunt Reenu kept this a secret from their maid Parvathy and other close ones. To them the reason was, that Alphy had a severe urinary tract infection, was under medication and resting for a couple of weeks as per doctor's advice.

Alphy spent long periods in the bathroom. She kept forgetting to change her pad. She was bleeding profusely like a damaged, leaking pipe. Alphy couldn't stop it. She cried to see her baby as a stream of gushing blood. Aunt Reenu was continuously knocking at the door. She figured that the door was left unlocked.

She entered to see Alphy lying unconscious in the bath tub, in a pool of blood.

36

Bob requested Connector magazine to extend Alphy's leave for another week. They insisted for a medical certificate. As a matter of fact, an employee who has recently joined and moreover has not even completed her probation period, wouldn't get leave. But Mr. Amith Gautham considered her health issues and permitted sick leave for two weeks. But it had exceeded that now.

Amith informed Bob that either Alphy has to submit her medical certificate or rejoin within a week's time.

There was no news from anyone in Bangalore. Christina Aunty, Reenu nor Alphy.

Sheaba grew anxious and to left for Bangalore.

Alphy was admitted in a psychiatry ward when Sheaba reached at Dr Babitha's Hospital along with Christina.

Alphy smiled at her.

" Sheaba... Don't ever advice anybody to destroy the seed. The seed is everything. You only require little time a day to water the seed. But to destroy it is the worst decision you can ever make in your life!"

Alphy were under strong sedation and medication. Christina and Babitha aunty left Sheaba with her at the hospital room for a bit.

Sheaba held her hand. She just seized as if she was holding a kitten. It was the most comfortable suite in the hospital and resembled a five-star hotel room. Everything was fresh as a daisy! Fruits were placed on the side table along with a knife, a coffee maker, kettle and assortment of tea bags. Diet and low-fat sugar were lined on a blue tray beside the tea pot.

Everything seemed present except Sheaba's friend. She was totally spaced out.

Did I give her an untimely advice? Oh...God, I never imagined she would end up in the psychiatry ward. A rose blanket covered her IV line. Her easel and palettes were also kept in a corner.

It was a psychiatric ward with all sort of VIP facilities.

Will it ease the mental trauma?

37

Days elapsed gradually. Alphy was sitting in the balcony with Sheaba. She had been talking to Sheaba continuously about one thing or the other.

Often she cried profusely towards the end, leading to uncontrollable howls and shivers.

Sheaba did nothing. She was flustered and was not able to provide clarity to her beloved mate. She had been thinking about Bob. How embarrassing the situation will be when we both meet him back in Dubai.

He will not talk in critical situations. He just leaves the house and spend hours kneeling at church before the cross.

He advised Alphy to sit before Mother Mary and gaze into the eyes of baby Jesus.

Alphy didn't go. I didn't let her. According to me, she was carrying the cross. And I needed to free her from it. She never wanted her friend to go through all the humiliation and harassment from the so called societal norms.

Sheaba accompanied Alphy to the airport when she had to leave for Bangalore. She insisted that Alphy reveals everything to her mother and Aunt Reenu.

Alphy pointed at the hoarding in front of the Dubai airport exit bay. 'Al Zahra hospital.' A mother heavily pregnant at nine months, with a tiny foot imprint against her stomach.

"Your baby, born in heaven"

Slogans are sarcastic at times. What happens if a

baby is not allowed to be born, does it still go to heaven? Which is real and unreal, birth or death? The concept of heaven was one she never gave thought to before. Before, it never mattered.

She tried to console her worries. A women was transforming into a mother at the first attachment to the uterus lining. She could sense that something had changed inside her. Either a tingle or murmurs from within... She was certain that the new one is announcing his or her presence through a microphone.

She held onto the reason she had to defend her vulnerability.

But it was like giving water to a scapegoat and consoling it to be happy, with the promise to join it in heaven. It is the wicked way of human..To lure you into sin and then search for a justification for your brutality!

Devil is far better than that again, why do humans blame the devil for their own conscious deeds?

38

Abhi's name popped up in Alphy's inbox after ten years.

She had isolated herself in her room at Bangalore after the psychiatry trauma, therapy and medication.

Dr Babitha insisted that everyone gives her space and not to intrude into her routine. Let her sleep on the sofa coiled like a centipede. Let her scream when she wants to, or immerse in the bath tub for hours.

Babitha only wanted to ensure that she takes her sleeping pills on time every night. She had to sleep for at least eight to ten hours.

Alphy didn't eat much. She sparingly ate a few vegetables, namely carrot, cucumber and lettuce. She likes finely chopped beetroot mixed with vinegar and salt. Her tongue stained purple and went slightly pale due to the vinegar. Would it stain if it's organic? Vegetables don't have any permanent colours strong enough to decolourise the tongue. The culprits are the pesticides and preservatives used to prolong their life.

If you cut a ladies finger in half and see any worms in it, it is natural. That's what Aunt Reenu used to say. She is a spiritual monk. Everyone gets angry or frustrated in life; But not her.

She never gets upset or angry in any situations. She entrusts her confusions to the universal power when she meditates each morning and all worries disappear. At least that's what she says. Alphy joined her occasionally during her college days. Alphy did yoga with her. She taught her how to meditate. She has a peculiar beauty with an oval face and identical pearl white teeth with a yellowish shade. Whenever she smiles, her beauty radiates.

"Why are humans trying to attain divinity?' Alphy asked her out of curiosity.

She replied,

"Trying to be divine is impossible for any human. Once you absorb positive vibes, then you start to see Jesus' sacrifice for mankind from a different perspective. Your charisma radiates and you will be respected knowingly or unknowingly.

Divinity is a myth guddiya... You can define it according to your attitude."

"I think sex is an example for divinity. If you are mating with your partner who you love..."

Alphy paused for a while and then continued,

"No, there is a better way to explain it. You don't feel to be physically touched if your soul is not longing for that person. If you touch someone to solely quench your lust, you may enjoy the momentary pleasure, but it will end after one intercourse."

Aunt Reenu didn't reply. She always kept silent when I talked about sex.

Alphy decided to accept Abhi's apology of vanishing without trace. He confessed that he was scared to face her and he didn't have the courage to receive her cold stare.

He said that love turns you into an escapist at times. It is definitely not right to run away like a coward from a girl, but it is less painful to listen to her say no!

After the initial awkwardness, Alphy felt relieved to get back her teenage friend. The distance between Abhi and Alphy diminished swiftly.

She agreed to join him for dinner at his place. Alphy

didn't ponder too much on the invitation. She wanted to move on.

Move on, not from her life. Her life is perfect. She wanted to move on permanently from Ayaan, or flush him out completely from her body and soul.

That was not like her, she never visits any male friend's place when they are alone. Classmates often visited her house, and even stayed over to finish reports and projects throughout the night. They sleep on the couch and she sleeps with Aunt Reenu.

She was conscious about her attire while her male friends were present. Alphy wondered whether all these boundaries were necessary or was it absurd. Bob as usual didn't reply to this query when she shared it with him.

39

Alphy pretended to be her usual cheerful self as was she applying oil on her hair. It's been weeks now. She wanted to go for a refreshing spa and facial. She likes fruit facial, papaya and orange were highly refreshing and rejuvenating.

She spent a lot of time in her hot water bath infused with bath salts that she drew for herself. She brought that from Dubai during her Christmas holidays the previous year. It is rose scented, and possessed the ability to exfoliate negative energy.

Alphy observed her body after weeks. As a matter of fact, she couldn't notice anything since the day she received her positive pregnancy test results.

'Your legs are the sexiest, after your lips.'

Ayaan peeped into her bath tub. She keenly observed her legs from her toes to her thighs. He was very particular about her legs, and didn't want any black spots to ruin it.

' Please take care of your legs even when you grow old my habeebi...'

'And your golden flawless skin mesmerises me...',

"Don't look at me dear, your eyes are magnets. I'm afraid that I won't be able to detach from them forever..."

' Where did you get this exceptional face from?!

I can't take my eyes off of you! It is damn gorgeous. May Allah save you from evil sights my darling... "

'You know what Alph, even our height differences complement each other... if you were taller than this,

I wouldn't have fallen for you...!"

Ayaan's whispers from their most private moments echoed in her ears when she started to observe herself. She felt devastated.

Thoughts can be controlled or at least deviated. She finished her bath immediately and wanted to get ready for her date.

Did Abhi mentioned that it is a date? She considered it as a one. She firmly restricted her thoughts, wiped and wrapped herself in her navy blue bath towel. She likes the scent of her bath salt. She was thinking about Abhi. He may like it too.

"Men relishes the scent of women! Not your Gucci perfume habeebi. Your skin possesses a scent and its deadly. I am intoxicated by your scent!"

Alphy was annoyed at his thoughts entering with no permission, no matter how hard she tries to avoid it.

She smelled her underarms, just to know which scent he was referring to. He savoured it like a puppy whenever they mated.

Alphy was exasperated! This won't do. It's my thoughts, my body, my mind, my passion and my scent. He has nothing to do with it. Alphy re-assured herself.

40

Abhi sported long hair with a clean shave. He was wearing a dark blue vest along with a navy blue blazer and light blue jeans. It was a stark contrast from the younger Abhi.

Was this the same boy who disappeared without a trace? Only because his friendship deviated to love? After mailing a letter and was nervous to hear her reply. He was scared of the embarrassment and taunt by others. Was this the same guy?

She was observing Abhi very closely and was doubtful about his emotion towards her now. Did he have any other girl in his life?

"Do you have a girlfriend?"

Alphy was wondering how that question escaped.

He smiled. "Do you?" Abhi asked her back.

"Yes." She doesn't expect to say yes, but she did.

"Oh, who is the lucky guy? Is he from Dubai ? Your colleague perhaps?"

Abhi was talking continuously. She was wondering whether this much conversation was exactly needed. Is he pretending to be talkative, or an extrovert. She couldn't come to a conclusion.

"He is in Lebanon"

"Oh...wow! That's cool yaar. So is he on a business trip, or is he a migrated Arab local?"

"No, Abhi. He is from Lebanon. Lebanese Muslim."

"That's sounds cool. I always knew you would choose someone really crazy and special!"

She didn't want to continue that conversation. She felt uneasy. Abhi noticed her face turning colourless. She was holding the wine glass and touching the rim with her tongue. Seemed like very peculiar manners, but he noticed her tongue colour. It was light purple.

"What happened Alphy?"

"We are not together anymore."

She rose from her chair and moved to the edge of the terrace. Abhi had a beautiful villa in Gandhi Nagar. It is like a delightful beach cottage! But there is no beach nearby. Palm Island was surrounded by the blue ocean. The Yacht was as enchanting for a couple under the moonlight.

Alphy was shivering, she couldn't help her vagabond thoughts. Her eyes started watering. She went to Abhi and asked him to hold her in his arms. Abhi hugged her and she buried her face into his chest like she was searching for something there. She pulled him close with the need to be blanketed.

Abhi was patting her hair. He couldn't resist smelling her.

"Do you like my scent?" she asked.

Abhi passionately looked into Alphy's eyes.

He lifted her face gently and kissed her forehead.

'It's everything about you that I adore. You were always a mystery to me. But other than you my dear, there was nothing for me. I moved back to Bangalore with all the courage that I've been gathering since the day I left you!

I shifted to Bangalore only for you. But you had left by then."

He kissed her eyes, ears, fingers, hair. She held him tightly like a boat anchored at a safe shore, in the middle of a thunderstorm.

Abhi dropped her back at her apartment.

He was always crazy for bizarre vehicles. Earlier it

was his twin bird, and now it is a black Lamborghini. His favourite colour is black. She also likes black. Like him, she also fancies extraordinary events. She is an intro-extrovert. A dual personality like Abhi.

He was broadened by passion and asked if he could kiss her lips. Abhi caressed her cheeks, ran his fingers over her shoulder and across her lower back tenderly like a feather.

"Could you drop me home?" Alphy asked.

She was scolding herself on the way back.

What the hell was that? Why did my body feel so cold? The man next to me was extremely passionate, hot, handsome and with full of love... What was wrong with me?

Alphy asked Sheaba to book flights for her the very next day. Abhi is an innocent man who loves her immensely. She didn't want to hurt him.

He came to see her off at the airport. He thanked her for the previous night with a wholesome smile. It was the most splendid night of his life!

41

The third day after Alphy reached back in Dubai, she got a call from Fujairah. It was Abdullah. He had been trying to reach both of their phones. By both, he meant Alphy and Ayaan. She told him that they had been out of country for a month.

The news that Alphy heard was totally shocking. Raheem was arrested by the labor department. It was totally unexpected when the labor officers visited the fish market for thaftheesh. They had directly taken him to jail. Abdulla couldn't do anything to help him so far.

Alphy started for Fujairah with an inevitable urge to see Nabeesa, Shabana, Nujoom, Athif, Zamina and Asker.

She didn't disclose her reason to Sheaba or Bob. She took her Polo and left early in the morning. Sheaba might enter her room to awaken her with a hot cup of coffee as usual.

The journey to Fujairah was not pleasant this time. A dust storm erupted out of the blue. The desert never reveals its mystery. The climate changes are the greatest examples.

If in the morning, it is raining, the evening will be sticky hot! The transition from hot to cold weather, is demarcated with rain.

Alphy forgot to charge her phone the previous night and it switched off as she was reaching Raheem's villa. Sheaba couldn't do anything when she heard that Alphy had left for Fujairah. She hated Fujairah! That journey ruined her friend's life. Bob asked Sheaba not to bring it up anymore. Let the past be.

But Sheaba couldn't forget it that easily. She hated Ayaan like never before. She cursed him. She knew that Alphy wouldn't do that, even if he betrayed her a hundred times, humiliated her, or even stabbed her with a knife. Sheaba couldn't understand why this girl stands mute. Did she enjoy being a victim?

A bold, confident well-known celebrity with a huge fan following, who stands up for women's rights, earning pretty good money, with social influence, breathtaking beauty, emotionally available, and to conclude, an extensively lovable person!

He disappears for more than six months to a year from her without any reason. Even if there is a stupid reason, the partner has every right to know. She recalled the times Alphy packed her bags to go and spend time with him, but unpacked everything after his last minute cancellation.

She would then cancel her leave and the pre booked tickets. And go to work with a blank face. How could a man keep his mouth shut and hurt his girl so brutally? No phone calls , no messages for an entire year... yet this girl opens her door for him!!

How could she keep herself numb? Why is she not reacting against him?

Love has to be fearless. If someone loves you, they should respect you also. They should have the commitment to not break a woman's heart. Sheaba never agreed to this brand of persistence. She never believes in surrender leading to self-torment.

She believed love is to be loved and to love. Love needs mutual trust and respect to survive.It was not a one-way bridge with access in only one direction.

But Sheaba couldn't hurt Alphy by saying all this. Even Bob agreed. Suppressed and unanswered questions burned inside Sheaba!

Bob didn't ask Alphy anything when they reached back from Bangalore.

He enquired about her mom and aunt. She was silent and talked about how the climate is unbearable in Bangalore these days. She talked about the pollution and the ignorant littering. How recklessly people drive there and how police tow cars parked along the roadside, later arguing with the owner for bribes. It's a pity when you see a police officer acting like a street beggar.

Alphy sighed, 'The roads were safe for parking before.She praised the Dubai police for their decency and graciousness. They always greet 'assalamu alaikum' when they arrive at an accident spot or any other violent area. Aren't they ?

They respect ladies and never ask a woman to exit the car, even if they are involved in traffic related incidents"

Alphy was talking continuously . Sheaba and Bob listened quietly.

At midnight, when bob returned from his office, he saw a figure at the living room balcony. It was 2 am and there was no light inside the hall. Bob went to see Alphy laying there on the couch. She looks like a centipede.

She lifted her head and saw Bob standing there. He sat next to her quietly. She got up and leaned on his shoulder .

"Bob, I couldn't save my baby..."

She said in a feeble voice and cried like a grieving mother who wept over the body of her child.

Bob sat there silently.

42

Alphy reached in front of Raheem's villa.

She didn't ring the calling bell. She knew how gravely they were frightened by calling bells. Poor children might be scared from the day they were born. The siren from a police car or ambulance; Even if someone was shouting from the nearby alleys, they hid instantly even if it was daylight. They were scared of sunlight, they were scared of moonlight. They were scared of every unusual sound that existed out of the ordinary. Bells intimidating them to hide inside their single room where the water was leaking from the roof. Oh... can't even imagine!

Nabeesa covered her children in a blanket. Like a hen, shielding her chicks from the eagle. Raheem was helpless when he saw the fear in his children's pale faces. He severed the connection to the bell. They have nobody who will come visit. They have nowhere to go. They cannot send their eldest daughter to a grocery to buy sugar, milk or samooli (bread rolls) in case of an emergency. They have plenty of time at home. Their home is their school, their play area, their market, their park, their road, their crowd, their city; their sky and soil.

Everything was within the four walls of their villa compound. Poor Shabaana used to picture the clouds as waterfalls, waves, and even heaven...!

Nabeesa was always frightened about the captivity of jail. It was better to be captivated here within the four walls of their villa with her husband and children for eternity. She cried when she thought about the separation. Raheem would be in the men's jail, me and the girls will be in the female prison. Would we be together or separate? And what about my little boy Athif? He is not even a man yet.

She surrendered her distressed thoughts to Allah, who is the most beneficent and merciful.

The children were trained to not make noise. They competed with each other on who will remain more quiet. The elder children won all the time. Baby Athif couldn't recognise the danger set in his failure and he wasn't bothered either.

Alphy was anxious. The gate is still locked. She tried the three-knock pass code again.

Her heart was palpitating with anxiety. Were they not there ? Did any of their friends take them home, maybe.

The gate squeaked and opened. Little Shabaana was hiding behind the gate door. She saw Alphy and asked her to come in quickly. Alphy entered and immediately closed the gate.

Shabaana was weeping as she pulled Alphy inside.

"Aunty, ummi is sick. Please help her!"

She murmured.

When Alphy entered into the bedroom, she was shattered.

Nabeesa was on the bed, her lower body drenched in blood, the kids surrounded her and were crying feebly.

"Alphy..."

Nabeesa raised her hand towards her,

"Save my baby. I'm bleeding..."

Alphy suddenly grabbed her phone to call the ambulance, but Nujoom stopped her.

"Aunty please don't call the police, they will put us

in jail like abba...”

Alphy switched off her phone. She went and held Nabeesa’s hands, Nabeesa was trying to say something. she couldn’t understand.

Alphy heard only one thing “save my baby!”

Alphy’s thoughts wandered at the sight of the pool of blood. She saw herself in the bathtub.

Alphy snapped back to reality and she asked Nujoom to take the other kids to the next room.

Alphy assured them that their ummi will be safe.

“Aunty will take care of her. All of you stay calm and please pray. Let Shabaana stay with me to help.”

The children nodded and went to the next room.

Alphy didn’t know what to do. Suddenly she recalled the assignment she had done during her journalism course about ‘Labour and Child Welfare in Tribes.’

Abhi was her partner and they had spent days and nights amongst the tribes. Most of them still do not opt for medical help during the pregnancy period and child delivery. Infants die due to complications during the delivery and the mothers because of heavy bleeding. They are still uneducated about the consequences. Alphy tried to recollect the delivery that she had witnessed at the aid of a tribal midwife in their hut. The thatched roof was made with palm leaves and tied together with sturdy bamboo sticks.

Alphy looked around and saw a plastic mat in the corner. She propped up Nabeesa’s legs in labour position. She kept the plastic sheet under her buttocks.

“Shabaana...’ Alphy asked, “Can I get few tissues or a clean towel ?”

Shabaana nodded her head, opened a wall cupboard and took out a bag. She opened the bag and it was filled with various emergency first aid provisions. Cotton, clean clothes, Dettol, and even kids towels.

'Abba usually keeps everything ready at home for ummi's delivery. ' Shabaana told Alphy.

Alphy wiped all the blood and asked Shabaana to bring a bowl of clean warm water.

Alphy's eyes filled with tears, when she saw the baby's head almost penetrating from her vagina! Her hands started shivering. Shabaana handed her gloves. And Alphy asked Nabeesa to push! Nabeesa was almost unconscious. But Alphy urged her to stay wake and start pushing.

"The head is almost here, Nabeesa. Please be strong!"

Nabeesa started screaming with pain, but immediately she suppressed her scream. Alphy cried to see her helplessness. Pain equivalent to death yet this lady is not allowed to scream.

Was the pain and scream aware of her illegal residence. Can emotions sense the physical boundaries of a human? Do they know of borders and territories, the documents needed to travel, and to reside in different countries?

Mother Mary... help us!

Alphy prayed continuously.

The baby's head and body came accompanied by a shriek into Alphy's hand. The new born was giggling with a cry! Shabaana had laid out a mat covered by a plastic sheet for the baby.

Nabeesa called out to her,

"Alphy... cut the cord."

Alphy saw the red tube stretching from the vagina connected to the baby's belly.

Alphy didn't know where to cut.

Nabeesa could see the fear on her face. It is the most crucial moment, if the cut is imprecise, the baby won't survive.

Alphy couldn't bring herself to take that risk.

Nabeesa requested her to go to the yellow and green colored Pakistani grocery. The family is close to Raheem, and they are trustworthy. Please inform that man to send his wife along with you.

Alphy got up, but her dress and hands were soaked in blood! Shabaana gave Nabeesa's Abaya to her.

Alphy threw it on and ran to the grocery. The man wearing long kandhura saw her terrified face. She informed him that Nabeesa requested whether his wife could help them. He asked her to wait for a minute and went through the back exit of the grocery. Their house was behind the shop.

A tall, beautiful lady wearing an abaya came along with him. Alphy pointed out that they might need a pair of clean scissors. Her husband handed her a new scissors from the shop. Alphy was not sure whether this one could be used. Surgical scissors and blades were more specifically crafted for their function.

When they reached back, Shabaana was holding the new born who was covered in blood, to her chest in her small hands.

"Fareedha..." Nabeesa called her helplessly.

"Assalamu alaikum Nabeesa. Sab teek ho jaayega. Please relax..."

she stroked Nabeesa's forehead. "Allah will take care.."

Fareedha tied the umbilical cord and then cut it at the mark. She put a small clip on it. She handed the baby to Alphy.

"Mashallah... it's a boy! Alhamdulillah..."

Fareedha raised her hands and thanked God Almighty.

Nabeesa was weeping, her lips were shivering, it was shrivelled without water. 'Raheem was so sure it would be a baby boy!'

Alphy looked into those little eyes. She wiped his

pretty face with clean wipes and then his whole body with a clean, wet towel. Shabaana gave her a baby towel to cover the baby.

Alphy wrapped up the little one. The very moment Alphy saw his sparkling eyes, ever so wide lined with eyelashes!

Did the infant smile at her?! Alphy shivered.

She felt his soul.

43

Alphy returned the next day from Fujairah after the sacred experience she witnessed. She couldn't stand there seeing the infant's dark grey eyes. She felt the same chocking; at the operation table.

Alphy was howling as she cried. Sheaba was holding her tightly.

"I lost my baby. I shouldn't have done that Sheaba.. Did I kill my baby? Oh God... how could I do that ?"

"Alph... please stop crying dear... God will never punish you for this. That lebanee will be at the brunt of it. It's not your fault my dear. Please don't curse yourself."

"But it was in my stomach Sheaba. I could have saved him, if I had tried! I shouldn't have bothered about Ayaan and his problems. I should have listened to Bob."

She cried louder and louder. Bob was not at home. Sheaba was crying with her too.

44

Alphy went to meet Gautham at Connector two days after her journey to Fujairah.

She informed him that she is going to quit. She said she couldn't complete the screening mission at Connector.

Gautham remained quiet. He knew that she was lying. What he didn't know was the reason. That she was lying to save a family who is residing illegally in the UAE for years. She called that humanity. To save them from imprisonment is a higher priority for her than a high profile job. For the company, it is just a breaking news, but for Alphy, they are her family now. A new born was also added to the family tree by her own hands, right in front of her eyes.

She still felt the baby's cheek pressed against her hand, his sparkling little eyes and his smile when she wiped him with wet tissues.

Sheaba was quiet when she heard Alphy's decision to leave Dubai for good.

"I won't be happy here anymore, Sheaba. I have to go."

Bob entered Alphy's balcony, the day before her journey to Bangalore. He showed her the newspaper; Al bayan in his hand for the very same day May 26, 2002

"AMNESTY FOR ILLEGAL IMMIGRANTS TO BE ANNOUNCED SOON

By Our Staff Reporters.

The UAE is set to announce an amnesty, for illegal

immigrants to encourage them to leave and avert prosecution in a drive to restore social and labour order, Lt. Gen. Dr Mohammed Junaid Al Bakhi, Minister of Interior, said yesterday.

Alphy looked up bewildered at Bob's face from the news paper, he smiled and asked her to continue reading.

" Dr Al Bakhi said the ministry had already studied , and hoped embassies in the UAE would help in its implementation.

The decision to give an amnesty for illegal residents reflect the country's tolerance in dealing with others, as all violators will be allowed to leave, as was the case a few years ago.

Interior ministry sources estimated that more than 150,000 violators of residence rules are staying in the country, most of whom were sneaked into the country via sea.'

Mukthar's beach villa security popped into Alphy's mind.

This is ridiculous! Won't Ayaan ever leave me alone? Alphy forcefully brought back her focus to the news.

'We are confident that embassies and consulates of several countries will cooperate with us in this regard as this will have a positive impact on their country as well. We hope the other middle east countries will follow this humanitarian initiative.

The UAE is providing all possible services and facilities to residents and expects them to comply with the laws of labour and residence. It cannot tolerate violation of laws.

Dr Al Baakhi acknowledged the infiltration problem but said UAE had taken counter - measures including tight security and surveillance at borders and coastlines, stringent penalties against employers of illegal residents and regular raids on suspected labour sites.

UAE government had launched a favourable initiative, it was a first in the Middle East.

It will definitely prove to be a blessing for residents staying in the country illegally for years. Most of them had accepted it as their fate. They thought either they will land in jail, or they will die as an illegal resident at their home eventually.

Without a visa nor passport, they can return to their home land. That's what AMNESTY is, an out pass of forgiveness to leave past without retribution.

Alphy's face changed, she hugged bob, he patted her shoulder with a smile.

45

Bob and Alphy went to Fujairah Central Jail to see Raheem. It was not as easy as they expected. Bob's prestigious client, Sheikh Nashid bin Sulthan Al Vahaab, Head of Defence in UAE , had to put a special note to the jail superior.

The jail complex was huge. They made their way through a long path way, with black, brick walls on either side. A policeman wearing an olive green uniform accompanied them.

They entered a large hall, where steel bars lined the adjacent wall. People from different nationalities were waiting in the hall. The police man asked Alphy and Bob to stay as close as possible to the steel bars and look into the hall behind the bars. Alphy saw a similar hall on the other side, filled with a huge crowd. They are eagerly looking towards to where Alphy and Bob were standing. They were in the visitors' area. The prisoners and visitors had to identify each other and converse loudly to be heard.

Alphy's eyes were straining to find Raheem in the crowd. She had met him only once. And Bob didn't even know him. Suddenly, she heard someone screaming her name. Raheem was waving and calling her name louder and louder from the prisoners' crowd.

Alphy was relieved to see him. Everyone was screaming to be heard. It was like noise polluted the cry of despair. Alphy couldn't make out a single word from the noise. Desperation made things worse. Is this the way they see each other? The prisoner and his visitor?

People are handing over food, some of them are

passing letters. Three or four policemen were standing in the middle of the two halls. Bob passed a note to Raheem with the help of the policemen.

Alphy had written about little Inaam! His family is safe along with the baby. She wrote about Amnesty and they are trying to get him and his family an out pass from United Arab Emirates to their home country.

Raheem cried when he read the note. Alphy could vaguely make out his face in the crowd.

Alphy saw that Raheem was trying to write something wedged between the crowd. He raised his hand and asked Alphy to wait for a while. Alphy received two pieces of paper through the police officer, she opened the first one to read.

Dear Alphy,

In the name of Allah, most beneficent and merciful, thank you for coming here bearing the wonderful news of my son's birth! I was totally lost till this moment as I was unaware about the whereabouts of my family after I was caught by the police. I cannot imagine how Nabeesa must have handled the delivery without me. I have taken two of our children's delivery by myself you know.

And I am grateful to know that they are safe with you.

I am thankful to Allah the almighty , for Amnesty . And may he bless you always for guarding my children and wife.

If I don't make it out of jail, please do help them to exit the country!

Hope Ayaan bhai is also doing fine.

Love Raheem.

Alphy turned over the second piece of paper. She saw Nabeesa's name on it. She didn't read it and showed a thumbs up to Raheem. It seemed like the letter was written long back, may be the day he was pushed into jail.

When Nabeesa opened the letter, her heart was ticking like a huge clock.

My dear Nabeesa,

Assalaamu alaikum dearest wife. I could imagine your state of mind when you heard the news of my arrest.

Life is Allah's gift and he knows how to handle it. At times, we humans can't see what's in store for us.

Something horrible happened, my arrest, but now it is going to turn into a good thing. It's our life boat, Alphy and Ayaan bhai are the sailors.

I couldn't sleep on August 9th, your delivery due date. Felt like my body was splitting into two, thinking of my abandonment during the most needy moment.

I was screaming inside these four walls when I thought about Shabaana, Nujoom, Athif, Zamina and Asker witnessing the delivery.

Finally I surrendered to Allah, who saved us all these years, believing that he will save you and my children in this desert .

Sorry Nabeesa , for all these years of suffering, for the only reason that you got married to me.

And take care of yourself and our children, wherever you may be, I am always with you.

I whispered 'baank' and 'Kaamath' in our little boy's ear on August 9th.

Kisses to you and our children.

Lovingly yours,

Raheemka.

Nabeesa cried with astonishment when she read the letter. She grew more surprised when she read the date he mentioned about the baby. It was the very same day little Inaam was born!

46

Abdulla helped Nabeesa, to handover whatever documents they had with them to Alphy. They tried to file for Raheem's plea.

Clearance from the court was needed to be obtained prior to availing the amnesty scheme. Only overstay issue will be considered by the UAE immigration.

Another hindrance was obtaining documents for their children who were minor and born in UAE and has not been registered with the UAE health authorities. Raheem and Nabeesa, the parents of the children, should register a complaint with the local police, then complete a DNA test to verify their parentage, after which the necessary travel documents will be issued for the minor.

Bob tried to make use of his contacts. They got the permission to do the DNA test . Raheem underwent the test from jail through the medical team. Alphy took Nabeesa and the children to Al Zahra hospital.

"Why are we here ummi?" Little Asker asked Nabeesa.

"We have to do a blood test before we go to Kerala dear."

"What is the blood test ? How are they doing it?' 'Asker continues.

"This is a hospital Asker...please be silent" Shabaana answered.

She knew her ummi was exhausted with all these processes.She had seen her mother crying after reading Abbu's letter the previous day.

“But we have never been to a hospital shabbu dheedhi”, Asker was very impatient.

“We have to see a doctor, check our blood and go home. Then the government will give us an out pass to exit from the country. We can go home finally. Aren’t you happy for that ?”

“Yes, but what about Abbu? Will he be coming with us ? I don’t want to leave Abbu alone and go to Kerala. I want to go to our old home in Fujairah, and wait for Abbu to return...”

Every one kept silent for a moment. Alphy took Asker and Athif along with her to a vending machine, and put coins in to buy chocolates and juice. They were excited to see the juice and chocolates move inside the booth! Little Athif asked whether he could try once, she allowed. He was overjoyed when the juice was dispensed with a sound. Alphy showed them how to collect their newly attained goodies from the booth. They put their hands in and took it out.

Asker forgot about the hospital conversation. He ran to his sisters and shared the juice and chocolates with them.

He started explaining about the functioning of the booth with wide eyes! They were listening curiously.

The blood tests were done and the results will be ready within a week’s time. They returned to Al Moosa tower.

47

Alphy wrote an article on Raheem and his family. It was her first assignment for Connector. She didn't want to publish it before merely for securing her job. But now that she had a security for their life; the intention was to grab maximum public attention so that they can touch the real sky!

Amith Gautham was astounded to read her article! The way the family had suffered, within the confines of four walls, for more than a decade. He even cried when he read the segment on Nabeesa's delivery, how she had swallowed her scream! How the children grew palpitated and terrified when they heard the police siren within proximity. How Raheem quietly concealed himself behind the huge waste bin, whenever officials visited the fish market.

Amit Gautham entered Alphy's cabin. She was surfing on her lap.

Alphy saw Amit's face, it was very pale. Amith hugged Alphy and said;

"It is you Alphy Ron, who brought that little boy into this world! I can't even imagine the traumatic situation you all went through. This story is going down in the history of Connector Magazine."

It was Alphy's face that went pale this time. She heard an unborn scream as she listened to Gautham's compliments.

The story appeared in Connector's tabloid. It was the talk of the town!

Amit asked Lily, the tabloid reporter and Omar, the

official photographer to assist Alphy to cover Amnesty news. Ayaan had taken few pictures on his camera on the day they met at Fujairah, some of which she had transferred to her laptop. It helped considerably.

Ayaan keeps revisiting each and every corner of Alphy's mind. No matter how hard she tries to block him out.

Sheaba asked her to concentrate on helping Raheem's family. Even Bob agreed.

The controversial story of Raheem and Nabeesa along with their six children appeared across various newspapers and TV channels.

But the exclusivity of the story and photographs belonged to the celebrated journalist, Alphy Ron. Reporters wanted to meet Alphy and know more about the family. They were curious to know about little Inaam's birth. The nerve wrecking situation that Alphy had tackled!

Alphy had no interest in any of that. She started to paint again.

The subject was a pearl diver, who fetches the pearl from the deep sea, and had oysters lining his head forming a hallow ...

Sheaba saw the painting portrayed on the easel when she brought Alphy her morning cup of coffee. It was not there the previous night. Sheaba knew since she was in Alphy's room until midnight.

Alphy was asleep on the couch, with brushes and a palate on her side table filled with an assortment of fresh paint.

So the course of the night created the pearl diver. It was mesmerising.

48

Bob and Abdulla were trying their best to obtain the court plea for Raheem. It was the Shari'ah law that, in an Arab country, a criminal sentenced to capital punishment can be discharged from jail, if he is forgiven by the victim's dependent.

Raheem's lawyer Mr Khaleel Mushtaq Al Hamidi, is one of Bob's best friends in Dubai and soccer game mate at Al Nasr Leisure Land Club.

He asked Bob and Abdulla to convince Raheem's sponsor at any cost as it was the only way for Raheem to be pardoned. If Raheem's old sponsor agrees to withdraw the case against him, the government would have no issues to release him.

There were thousands of Indians who were residing illegally in UAE for years. The number was comparable for other nationalities as well.

Government started an exclusive division to move proceedings under the supervision of emigration department. Huge, white tents were set up. Heavily embroidered golden lace fabric which was hung inside the tent. Neatly aligned white chairs filled the hall. At the rear, police officers are sitting in a row with computers and necessary files on their desk.

Volunteers from different colleges and community groups were making their way through the crowd, and helping the people who were confined within four walls, immersed in utter darkness for years. They did not even know how to fill the forms. Some of them even had forgotten when they had arrived in the country for the first time.

High ranking officials and emigration executives were present round the clock. Water and snacks were offered to the applicants.

Alphy was amazed at their hospitality. These immigrants were residing in their country illegally. Moreover, they had committed a severe crime which was punishable until yesterday!

Few people still had insecurity reflected on their faces and grew tense whenever they saw a police officer. For a majority of their time, whom they were scared to death of.

Alphy and Bob collected the exit pass from the Indian embassy. Bob's former colleague, Mr. Sharaf, who at present is actively involved in social service, was at hand to assist them to clear the embassy paperwork.

Alphy thanked Mr Sharaf for his timely help. He was a fan of Alphy's articles.

He was trying to help illegal emigrants from Kerala, especially families like Raheem and Nabeesa.

"Miss Ron, it's a great pleasure to assist you. I have been reading all your articles, and every one of them are outstanding and highly brave! Your social commitment and kindness is remarkable. What I admire the most is even though you would have lost your job at Connector, you didn't publish the story initially. You were more concerned about their well-being than your own career or personal gain."

Bob laughed, "Alph, he is such a liar. There is no one in UAE like him. He is always striving for others even if it jeopardises his own family."

Alphy smiled at him. Sharaf nudged Bob's shoulder and smiled at her subtly and replied,

"Dont mind him Miss Ron, he is talking about my family. Isn't that right you bloody...artist?

Miss Ron, my wife went back to Kerala, because of my over social commitment. That's what he intends to point out..."

Sharaf laughed, but Alphy couldn't join his laughter. She felt uneasy.

Alphy was preoccupied on their way back home. What is more important? Happiness of your close ones or social services?

If someone dedicates himself to support others without understanding their own family or friend's needs, then who is there for them in their vulnerable moments...?

49

Nabeesa's and the children's documents were cleared faster than they had anticipated. But in Raheem's case, things were more complicated. His sentence and penalty, for illegal residence for more than twelve years, was huge and the arrest took place before amnesty was declared. Therefore, it has to go through court and follow the legal procedure.

His sponsor had filed a case against him stating 'forgery' and 'absconding'. He had also submitted Raheem's passport at Umm Al Quwain police station.

The closing date was near. Alphy and Abdulla with the help of Bob's strong influence tried their best to persuade Raheem's sponsor to withdraw the forgery case. But he didn't agree.

Nabeesa heard the disappointing news from Alphy. They were at Bob's apartment.

She couldn't think of leaving the country without Raheem! They were together, in their fight for life, the hunger, the sickness, the pain, the terrifying moments while being on the run constantly! Raheem protected them like a blanket through those miserable years.

The day before their flight, Nabeesa told Alphy, that she wanted to meet Raheem's sponsor at Umm Al Quwain. When Abdulla heard her request, he immediately disagreed.

"It is not a good idea Nabeesa. What will we do if the sponsor hands you over to the police?"

Sponsor Ibrahim had no clue that Raheem's family is still here in UAE.

Bob heard about Nabeesa's request and determination. He said she should give it a try if she believes strongly that it will help Raheem.

Nabeesa said, "I have faith in Allah. I should at least try and leave the rest to him."

They went to Umm Al Quwain along with her newborn son. The rest of them stayed back with Sheaba. Nabeesa asked the children to pray.

The sponsor was furious to see Nabeesa! He shouted at Abdulla.

" How dare you to bring her here ? Do you want her also behind bars along with her kids ?"

Abdulla tried to explain the situation but it was of no use. Arabaab was too furious to listen to him.

"Assalaamu alaikum sir, my name is Bob Justin, I have my own advertising agency in Dubai, it's an LLC with high end clients. I can assure you on behalf of Raheem, that I would pay the amount Raheem owes you. You can keep my passport as security until I settle it. Please show some mercy to the family and Raheem. They have suffered enough."

Alphy was astonished at the way Bob spoke to the sponsor. He was determined yet calm.

Nabeesa looked at Bob with tears in her eyes. Who are these people ? Are they really humans or angels sent by God? They don't have any connection with my family. Even close relatives and friends didn't show any compassion to the family.

Instead strangers, like Fareedha and her husband back in Fujairah, with their single shutter grocery shop fed my children when we were hungry. Abdulla, who has there for us whenever we needed him. He brought Alphy and Ayaan to us. Now through Alphy, came Bob and his wife Sheaba. And other people who tried to clear our documents on time. Sharaf, Lily and Omer, even Amit Gautham who assigned the story to

Alphy to research on the illegal immigrants.

The dots connect when we look backwards. Every single thing that happens, happen for a purpose in this universe.

Bob offered his passport again as security until they pay back the money Raheem owed. Alphy requested to give him some more time to pay it.

The sponsor's attitude didn't change. He threatened that he would include Nabeesa's name in the forgery case.

Nabeesa didn't say a word, she was listening quietly through the entire conversation. Little Inaam was asleep on her shoulder. He awoke in-between when he heard Ibrahim shouting. Inaam started crying and everyone grew quiet.

Ibrahim asked Nabeesa to sit down and he further requested her to go inside the villa and pick a room to feed the baby. She politely declined.

'Assalaamu alaikum ya Arabaab.'

She enquired about his wife and twin boys.

She praised the UAE government's generosity towards expatriates, and how they had offered amnesty. They can fly back now, and her children can finally see their homeland , their grandparents.

At last, her children can go to school.

"We didn't sleep peacefully for a single day from the moment you filed the case against Raheem. It has been more than twelve years. Yet I always wished and prayed for a peaceful life for you and your family. Only you can help us in this critical situation. If you aren't willing ; let me surrender it to Allah, the Almighty. Mahassalaama ."

Nabeesa rose from her chair and started to leave.

Alphy glanced at the sponsor one last time and asked,

"With all respect sir, would you please think about

the total scenario? What was the reason behind the absconding and forgery cases of Raheem? Please justify with yourself what exactly the reason was to put Raheem in jail.

Not for us, but for your peace of mind. To make sure that you will sleep well even after years pass."

Nabeesa took hold of Alphy's hand gently. Alphy was shivering as she concluded her talk.

On the way back to Dubai from Umm Al Quwain, Nabeesa looked out through the car window. She saw the desert for the last time.

She remembered the painful night when they left behind their shop of livelihood , the villa they had lived in from the day she arrived in the gulf. Their early honeymoon period, first pregnancy, first born's footsteps in their villa compound in Umm al Quwain.

Memories flooded into Nabeesa's mind.

joy, the togetherness, the cry of their first born, she couldn't forget even a single moment.

She could still hear Raheem's friend, Khalid whispering as they were hiding inside the car travelling with him to Fujairah.

"Sandstorm! Ya Allah, no one can predict the weather change in the gulf."

Her eyes were welling up. Glimpses of her were popping up without invitation.

Her *mehandhi* night back home, Kannoor...

Friends were playing *oppana*, relatives were putting henna on her hands... every one was happy and enjoying.

Nabeesa was just eighteen. Raheem entered to the *panthal* with his relatives and friends. He looked handsome in a white dhoti and white shirt, with a white kerchief covered on his head. He had wore a long glitter string over his head.

Friends were teasing and laughing; Nabeesa could

still hear the laughter and excited conversation. " *puthyapla vannu..., puthyapla vannu...*"

And there were the rush to see the Puthyapla, the bridegroom.

50

Nabeesa and the kids were ready to go to airport. She did not want Alphy and her friends to undergo any more stress because of her family. She came to this desert holding Raheem's hand with a joyful and dancing heart. And now, after thirteen long years, she was returning without him along with their six children...

Bob informed that he was stuck with an important client and asked Sheaba and Alphy to drop them at the airport.

Everybody was silent while getting ready. Alphy and Sheaba were helping them to do the final packing. While filling toys and sweets into the bag, they noticed an old, black bag, lying on the floor, it was filled with Raheem's belongings.

The black colour had faded to pale grey as years passed... It was the first bag Raheem had brought with him when he first landed in this desert. Nabeesa had gathered everything from their home in Fujairah and brought it to Dubai.

Alphy noticed everyone eyeing the bag every once in a while with a solemn face. She saw tears in Zamina's eyes .

Alphy held her tiny hand and hugged her. "Honey, we will definitely help free your abbu from jail soon. We are all trying and will continue to, even if you are all back in Kerala. So don't worry. Be happy and go to your home country. "

The others were also listening to her intently.

Little Asker came closer to Alphy and she patted his head affectionately.

Sheaba was driving her Pajero. No one uttered a word on their way to the airport. Alphy looked through the rear view mirror at the kids' faces, and the emptiness reflected through their gestures. As they neared Sheikh Rashid flyover particularly designated towards the airport, they saw the huge sign 'Dubai international Airport' perched on top of the dynamically shaped, glass architectural marvel with segregated departure and arrival terminals.

When they reached the airport, everyone was wide eyed and looking around frantically. They looked like prisoners who were released after life imprisonment. But in their case, they were born as prisoners without committing any crime.

The children were carrying their small backpacks and the rest of the luggage were loaded onto a trolley; Raheem's old, grey bag rested on top of all, After that they entered the departure terminal.

Sheaba with everybody's out-passes and tickets approached the check-in counter, and the rest of them followed her. People who were travelling with out-pass from Amnesty had a separate counter at the airport.

Thousands of people were waiting at different counters designated to respective countries, their faces lit up with joy. Hundreds of kids, teenagers and middle-aged people who boasted a smile of relief that they could finally touchdown on their homeland, and live the rest of their days peacefully.

Police and airport special staff for amnesty were controlling the crowd and also assisting them with all their needs.

Alphy was standing across the check-in counter and observing them. Baby Inaam was sleeping on Nabeesa's shoulder peacefully. He is a lucky boy! He would be free in this world and also gifted freedom to everyone. He fulfilled his name 'Inaam'.

She saw Nabeesa's eyes wandering. Even the kids are gazing as if they are still waiting for someone to join their team.

Uncertainty is a curse. Human life itself is so uncertain and unpredictable . The pillar of their family is missing! They are forced to go back without him, even though they don't want to. He is still in jail and no one had a clue about his final judgement and how long it will take.

Getting a plea from his sponsor was the last hope, and that didn't work out.

They weighed their luggage and was checked in. Little Aathif was keenly observing their bags as it travelled through the conveyer belt.

Nabeesa's heart was beating furiously after she received the boarding pass in her hand. She desperately misses Raheem and her heart broke when she heard the zuhar prayer call.

Alphy and Sheaba hugged the children one by one. When Alphy hugged Little Asker he placed something in Alphy's hand and whispered in her ear.

"Aunt Alphy, could you please give this to Abbu?"

It was a piece of paper folded in half. She kept it safely inside her bag and promised Asker, "Definitely dear, I will. "

"When is he going to come ? I prayed a lot..." he asked with trembling lips.

"Your prayers will surely be answered Asker, don't worry. I want you to be strong and be with your mom and sisters.

Will you? Promise ?"

"Hm....mmm" he promised by placing his small hands onto her palm.

'Air India flight to Calicut ....'

First call for proceeding to immigration was being announced. Alphy asked everyone to get ready and proceed to immigration counter.

Alphy got a call from Bob says he reached at the Airport and asking where they were. She told him, they are still at the launch after checking, and ready to go inside for boarding.

All of them eagerly waited for him to come and say their final good byes.

51

Bob reached the airport.

Nabeesa, Sheaba and Alphy froze to see Raheem with Bob, and behind them Abdulla and Raheem's sponsor, Ibrahim.

Nabeesa cried with joy! The children were overjoyed to see their Abbu after two long months. Ibrahim handed out chocolates to the kids and said; " I have withdrawn the case against Raheem. Forgive me Nabeesa, for all the pain that I have caused you and your family"

Nabeesa kept her right hand over her chest and said. "shukran ya Arabaab" in a feeble voice. She praised Allah the Almighty in her heart.

"Forgive me Nabeesa, for all the pain that I had caused you and your family" Ibrahim said.

Nabeesa couldn't say a word more. She was literally crying. They wasn't tears of pain, but tears of joy!

"Allah will not grace a person if he is not kind and helpful to his own community!"

Ibrahim thanked Alphy for her words, which brought him out of his darkest place. He said he didn't know exactly what had happened to him at the time he filed the case against Raheem. It must have been money? Or the jealousy to see Raheem's growth in such a short span.

"No idea sister Alphy. But you are the kindest person I have ever met. You and your friends showed me what kindness is.

Shukran ya habeebthi, Allah will bless you all, and pray for me also, so that Allah forgives my sin."

"Assalaamu alaikum Ya Raheem", he hugged Raheem, with tears in his eyes.

"Va alaikummussalaam Ya Arabaab". Raheem wished him back politely.

Ibrahim shook hands with Bob and Abdulla and walked away.

52

On the way back from airport, Alphy recalled the first time she met the family.

They believed that Alphy and Ayaan had come to help them escape their house imprisonment. Alphy had longed and prayed to help them in some way.

God accorded amnesty.

Raheem and Nabeesa along with their six children flew back to their homeland.

Now, pray for a world with no borders and territories. Where humans could stay wherever they want. They can travel, stay, eat and meet with no manmade lines restricting them.

Alphy was completely silent on their way back to Al Moosa tower.

Bob didn't ask anything and Alphy didn't explain anything.

Sheaba was gazing out to the sky silently. Which is very rare considering she never keeps quiet for more than five minutes.

"Bob, do you believe in God?"Alphy asked in a feeble voice.

" Raheem's sponsor didn't take my passport as security to release and vacate Raheem's case.'

Alphy kept silent.

She was missing little Inaam. The name that Alphy had named him.

The children were excited when Alphy gifted them toys, dresses and sweets! She gave The Pearl Diver painting to Nabeesa. Alphy asked her to give it to little

Inaam as a gift from Aunt Alphy when he grows up and well enough to understand 'the hallow and pearls'!

Bob answered paradoxically.

"Do you want to challenge your God Alph? Challenge him. Tell him, that you want to be happy. Ask him to prove he exists"

53

Alphy had packed her luggage. She chose the Emirates flight at 1:30 pm. She likes to fly in daylight.

She likes snowy-white, floating clouds. Air turbulence during night flights makes her uneasy and sleepless.

All set to leave to her home town, Bangalore.

Amit Gautham requested her to stay; but had to accept her resignation when he understood that she was firm on her decision. He asked her to return whenever she feels the time is right, Connector's door is always open for her.

Alphy felt nostalgic for a moment while leaving Dubai. It has been five years, the city was nesting Alphy in her lap like a child. The City of Pearls!

She heard the song of the 'hauler', the singer coordinated the rhythmical chants to ease the vigorous pearl diving tasks, from sunrise till sunset.

She remembered the moment when Ayaan gifted her a jewellery set - pearl chain and pearl stud earrings. It was a pleasant surprise when they visited an island called Marwah, in Abudhabi.

It was an unexpected and hence unplanned trip, she couldn't even fetch her cloths. He picked her up from her office car parking lot and drove away.

When she received the gift from him, she was taken aback.

"This is unbelievable! You never believed in surprise gifts"

" This is not a surprise for me my dear, I have been waiting this whole year to get my bonus to purchase this for you. It's rare and expensive. So with the divine presence of the few scattered islands; May I ? "

He approached her with the pearl string in his hand.

"Why did you buy then ? I don't usually use ornaments."

"I know. You wear small diamonds pendants. Start using pearls from now. Because your future husband would like to see your pretty neck furnished with pearls"

Alphy shut her eyes tightly trying to erase the conversation.

She looked at Trade Centre which was just opposite of Al Moosa tower. She recalled the historical show they had put on for tourists, to learn more about the history of UAE.

They showcased a statue of His Highness Sheikh Zayd Bin Sultan Al Nahyaan, with an eagle perched on his hand, which was declared their National bird when the seven emirates united as one. It's a remarkable saga when the seven emirates united as one to build up the desert into a garden of prosperity with wealth and strength. Pearls to oil!

And their meticulous step by step brilliance in architecture, attracted people all around the world to UAE; especially to Dubai, Abudhabi and Sharjah.

Dubai Creek, Jumeirah beach, Mushrif Park, horse race , the biggest tennis tournaments sponsored by Dubai duty free; worlds number one duty free shop...

Alphy deviated her thoughts instantly. Whenever she thought about these places, someone else will pop up. He will walk with her , hold her hand, hug her, kiss her and call her name passionately...

Alphy heard Sheaba calling and returned her gaze

from the bustle of Sheikh Zayed Road.

Sheaba entered her room accompanied by a five year old girl with pretty blue eyes and rose petal cheeks. She was holding Sheaba's hand.

Sheaba told Alphy.

"Ayaan is here!"

54

Alphy saw Ayaan sitting on the living room couch. She spoke to him calmly. She had a chitchat with his daughter too.

"What's your name pretty young lady?"

"Zara Ayaan Ali." She replied in a soft and clear voice.

'That's a pretty name indeed. Just like you."

Alphy gave a shakehand to Zara.

"I am Alphy Ron..."

"I know you, Abbu told me everything about you!" Zara answered and looked up at Ayaan.

'Isn't it Abbu?'

Ayaan nodded his head .

Zara made her way towards the balcony. She touched the flowers and plants with affection.

Ayaan looked at Alphy.

Alphy asked, "How are you?"

He didn't reply to her question, instead he asked her to forgive him, and be with him if she can accept his daughter.

She smiled. She didn't want to drag this moment even for a minute. She was no longer a fan of vacuum.

"Every minute has it's own time! You never respected time Ayaan.

I could have forgiven you for the way you ignored my love and my pain. I could have forgiven you for abandoning me when I needed you the most. I could have forgiven you for concealing the real you from me.

I could have forgiven you, if you apologised for killing my baby, before you proposed to me at this moment."

Sheaba brought coffee and kept it on the white wooden coffee table in front of them.

Moments of utter silence were broken when Zara returned from the balcony with an innocent smile, Alphy patted the little girl's hair.

She then rose from the couch and walked to her room and closed the door .

oo

We cannot practice
detachment.
We can only practice,
how to attach to the light
Which will give us peace.
When you are in bliss,
the darkness from our life,
will detach
unknowingly

\- *Sufi*

ABOUT THE AUTHOR

Saheera Thangal was born in Palakkad, Kerala, daughter of Muthukoya Thangal and Aysha Beevi.

On completion of her bachelors in Botany, She migrated to Dubai, United Arab Emirates. There she joined an advertising agency, and also started pursuing Masters in Business Administration.

Life abroad broadened passion for reading and writing, moreover works were published by mainstream publications.

Her Debut poetry collection 'Njaan Enna ottavara' (Me, a single line)was published by DC books in the year 2007. In 2008, her well-acclaimed debut novel' Rabia' published, questioning the exploitation of Islamic polygamy and was debated across various platforms and gained an outreach. Aashramakanyaka (The Hermitage Maiden), Praajeenamaaya oru Thakkol (The Ancient Key), Vishudha Saghimaar (The Holy Muses), Olikkavithakal (The hidden Poems) and Oro vyakthiyum oro raajymaanu (Every human is a country) are some of her well read books.

Awards: Mahila thilakam award of Kerala Government, Young emerging writers award at Kovalam literary festival, Ankanam Sahithya Award, Gulf arts and literary award, Arabia Sahithya award, Malayalam News award.

Post Graduation in Business Administration (MBA) and Applied Psychology (MSc) and currently residing in Cochin, Kerala.

Actively involved in the field of Social work, Ms Thangal, is working as Faculty under Kerala

Government , Counsellor at Family Counselling Centre at Kerala High Court. Founder and Psychologist at Chrysalis Counselling and Consultants, Cochin.

Fb and instagram/saheerathangal